Contents

Message from Her Majesty The Queen

Christians and those of many other faiths in the United Kingdom and from around the world were united in celebration at this New Year marking the beginning of the third millennium since the birth of Jesus Christ. The year 2000 is a significant milestone for us all and a time of hope and optimism.

The great national exhibition housed in the Dome on the Meridian Line at Greenwich is a demonstration of our confidence and commitment to the future.

Within the largest enclosed space on earth are many examples of this country's inventiveness and imagination. The Millennium Experience, in the same tradition as its predecessors, the Great Exhibition of 1851 and the Festival of Britain in 1951, provides a focus for the nation's celebrations at an important moment in our history, bringing together people from communities throughout the United Kingdom and from many other countries.

I hope that your visit to the Dome is a memorable one offering a unique experience and an inspiring vision of life in Britain in the new millennium.

Elizabeth R
1 January 2000

The significance of the millennium

A baby is born – and your whole world changes. The birth of Jesus even changed how much of the world measures time. These millennium events recall that birth – like a two thousandth birthday party! While Christians will rightly be celebrating this anniversary, it is a significant moment for everyone of all beliefs to reflect on the past and look forward to the future.

The life of Jesus

So what is its connection with Jesus and why did he have such an impact? Jesus came from a poor Jewish family, living in obscurity under Roman rule. Aged about thirty, he left his daily work for the life of a wandering prophet, preaching the renewal of Israel. He proclaimed the 'rule of God' and taught people to pray to God as Father. He was particularly concerned for the poor, weak and marginalised. He healed people, bringing freedom, especially to women and 'outsiders'. In teaching the Jewish law, he stressed the commandments to love God and to love your neighbour as yourself. He attracted large crowds and engaged in vigorous debate, especially about his own role in the 'rule of God'.

The turmoil during his last visit to Jerusalem for Passover led to his arrest and execution. The Romans often crucified troublemakers – and their followers would soon disperse. Except that this time, they didn't. Within a few days, people were saying that his tomb was empty and they had seen Jesus alive. His frightened followers were so transformed by this experience that they turned the ancient world upside down, with many of them dying for their beliefs. Although, as Jews, they believed in only one God, their experience of knowing God in Jesus and through his Spirit led to their separation from Judaism and the Christian understanding of God as 'three in one'.

Within two hundred years, this conviction that 'Jesus is alive' reached even the distant British Isles. A century later Constantine, who was born in York, became the first Christian emperor of the Roman world. Christianity spread down the centuries and around the globe, changing even the landscape through the construction of churches and cathedrals.

What year will begin for other faiths in the year 2000?	
Bahá'í calendar	157 Bahá'í Era
Buddhist calendar	2544
Hindu calendar	2057 (Vikrami Samvat) or 5102 (Yugabda)
Jewish calendar	5761
Muslim calendar	1421 AH (After the Hijra)
Sikh calendar	531 Nanak Shahi Sammat
Jain calendar	2527 Vir Nirvana Samrat
Zoroastrian calendar	1379 (Fasli)

Unfortunately, it was also involved in persecutions and bloody wars. At the same time, many have been inspired by Jesus's example to continue his work of teaching, healing and liberating – all 'in the name of Jesus'.

Measuring time

When Jesus was born, time was measured locally by the year of a king's reign or the office of a priest. The common system across the ancient world counted years AUC, *ab urbe condita*, 'from the foundation of the city' of Rome. Five centuries after Jesus's death, Dionysius Exiguus (or 'Denis the Short') proposed counting from Jesus's birth, *Anno Domini*, 'in the year of the Lord', 533 AD. A thousand years later, this calendar was some days out from the solar year, so Pope Gregory XIII realigned it. This 'Gregorian calendar' is still used today – which is why this is the end of the second millennium from the birth of Jesus.

Different faith communities use other systems of dating (see list above). Despite these different dating systems, people of all beliefs have been planning millennium celebrations together, discussing their faiths and values. A good example of co-operation within today's multi-faith context has been the role of the Lambeth Group and the Inter-Faith Network in offering advice about the faith aspects of the Dome.

A millennium birthday party

It's all a long way from the birth of the baby Jesus, yet he continues to have this impact. Christians believe he is the Son of God; Muslims revere him as a prophet, while others – including Sikhs and Hindus – respect him as a religious teacher. Many of no religious belief are inspired by his human example of teaching, healing and liberating. Two thousand years later, this 'birthday party' invites us all, whatever our beliefs, to look back at the period since that birth – and forward to the challenge of the new millennium.

The Reverend Dr Richard A Burridge

Dean of King's College, London

Introduction

Welcome to the Millennium Experience.

By the end of the year 2000 the Millennium Experience – which includes the National Programme, the Millennium Festival and activities at the Dome – is likely to have involved forty million people. Seven million of them, like you, will have visited the Dome at the Prime Meridian in Greenwich.

The Dome was built to house an exhibition with appeal for everyone. What you see in the Dome was shaped by the opinions and wishes of thousands of people across the UK who told researchers what they wanted in their millennium celebrations. People wanted the Dome to address the challenges and opportunities we face at the beginning of the new millennium. These are issues common to people in all countries.

The contents of the Dome were developed around three broad themes – who we are, what we do and where we live – which are explored in fourteen zones. There is no set route around the Dome, which is like a small town with streets and open spaces between the zones. You can explore the Dome in the order which suits you.

Each zone was created by a different team of designers, artists, experts, engineers and architects, working under the management of the New Millennium Experience Company. The diversity of the subject matter and the range of different approaches taken by the designers has created a rich experience for the visitor.

The Millennium Experience is an expression of optimism and hope and will create a lasting legacy. The Dome will have a long-term impact on the local area through its own future use, the new transport infrastructure, the regeneration of the peninsula and the Millennium Village. Thousands of jobs have been created in the neighbourhood and people have been trained in new skills which will help them in their future lives. The Millennium Experience will have many other legacies around the UK through its National Programme, the Millennium Festival and its work with charities and schools.

The experience of visiting the Dome can open people's eyes to new ideas and show new products and policies at work. It can excite and inspire everyone, especially young people, while providing excellent entertainment. A day at the Dome should be an amazing memory for the rest of your life.

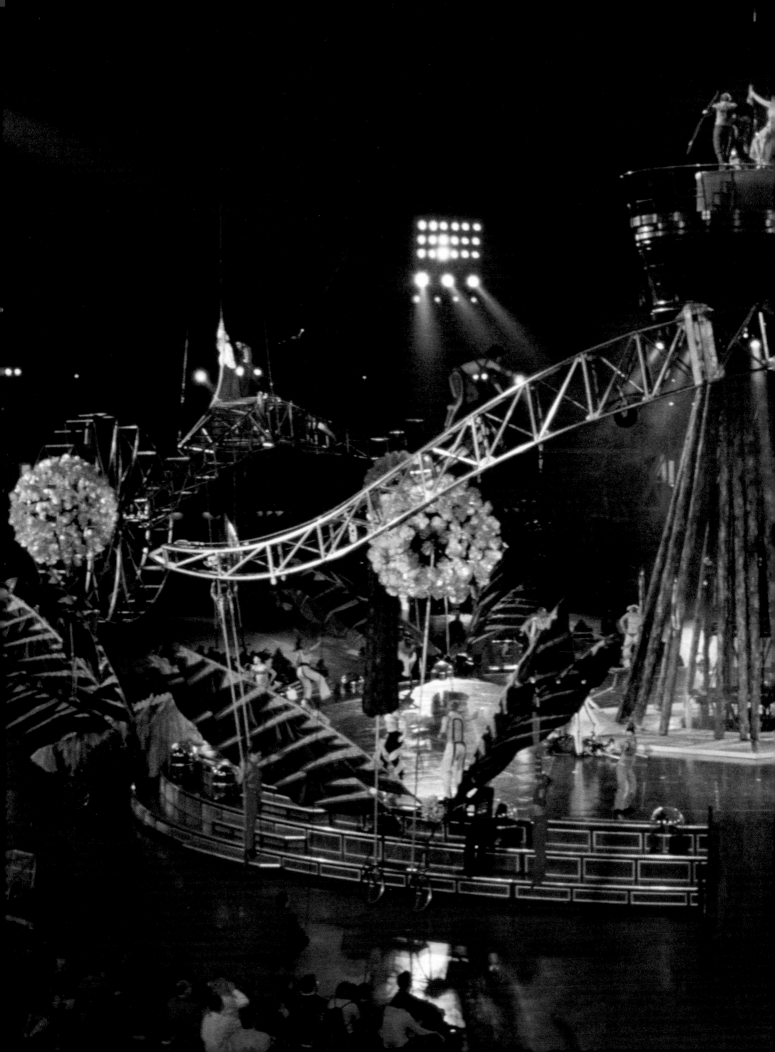

The Millennium Show

The central arena is a massive entertainment space at the heart of the Dome. Fifty metres high and the size of Trafalgar Square, this is also the home of the *Millennium Show*, a breathtaking spectacle of music, dance and aerial performance where performers bungee jump, spin, tumble and fly in the air, at heights of 50 metres and speeds of 30 mph.

Creative Director
Mark Fisher
Musical Director
Peter Gabriel
Artistic Director
Micha Bergese
Costume Designer
and 3D Props
Keith Khan
Lighting Designer
Patrick Woodroffe
Assistant Director (Aerial)
Andrew Watson

The Millennium Show weaves together elements of contemporary fable, historical allusion and powerful original music. It tells the dramatic tale of Skyboy – a boy of dreams and Sophia – a girl of action, who are driven apart before finally being reunited. It portrays a family divided by internal conflict and by the great changes in their worlds, as each generation struggles with the coming and passing of their own time.

At the heart of this timeless story is a family. The show tells of the father, Theo, who loves the earth and everything that grew from it. It tells of the mother, Beth, who could foresee the future, but was powerless to stop her family's destruction. It tells of the son, Ion, who harnessed technology to try to protect his father's changing world, but ultimately caused its ruin. It tells of the daughter, Sophia, whose quiet and enchanted childhood ends when she falls in love with one of the mysterious Sky people, defying her family. It tells of Skyboy, an outsider whose dreams turned from mischief and seduction to rebellion and love for Sophia.

Act I – In the beginning, the Sky people and Earth people play together in a natural world. Skyboy from the air and Sophia from the Earth, meet and fall in love. A violent storm shatters the harmony of their world and Theo, despairing at the wreckage, dies.

Act II – Earth boy Ion, asserts himself as the ruler of a changing world. This new era of technology and greed is symbolised by the construction of a giant iron tower and leads to conflict between the Sky and Earth people, separating the lovers. As Ion clings to the disintegrating structure, he is destroyed.

Act III – In the aftermath, Skyboy searches for Sophia; they meet and fly together as one. Their union brings together the liberated Sky and Earth people as a beautiful tree drives its way upwards from the ruins, a symbol of new life reaching out into an uncertain yet hopeful future.

The Company, specially created to perform this unique show, is divided into two casts. On stage at any one time will be up to sixtyone performers including soloists. In the spring of 1998, the Millennium Show production team auditioned over 3000 young people from across the UK to find ninety fit, keen and committed individuals who were willing to be trained for the show. Auditions were open to people with no previous performance experience. The Dome, in partnership with The Circus Space, the UK's premier circus training organisation, ran two six-twelve month long courses in aerial and acrobatic performance skills. This prepared the would-be performers for the challenge of executing complex flying effects with groundbreaking technology. The Dome also set up a technical

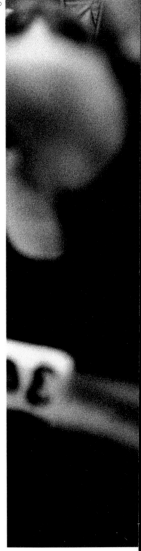

training program in lighting, sound, stage-management, costume, props and rigging for young unemployed people from southeast London. The Summer school, now in its second year, has filled a

The **Millennium Show** was conceived by **Mark Fisher** and **Peter Gabriel**

6

pp 10-11 The Millennium Show explores humanity and nature through three generations of a family

An intensive training programme included:

1 Learning to dance in the air on a cord lisse

2 Improving performance techniques

3 Developing physical stamina

4 & 6 Learning aerial skills

5 Over one hundred and sixty people from across the UK, Europe, the USA, Australia, Canada and Brazil were recruited at auditions held nationwide – Micha Bergese, Artistic Director, watches over

umber of full-time ositions within the how. Rehearsals moved o the Dome in eptember 1999. eventy ground-based erformers with xperience in physical heatre, dance and

mime and ten soloists joined the newly qualified aerial performers. For the next four months the one hundred and sixty two members of the Millennium Show Company worked together to create one of the most complex pieces of physical theatre ever staged.

This unusual approach to creating a show has established a group of performers keen to push at the boundaries of physical theatre. Their work at the Dome has positioned the UK firmly at the forefront of contemporary circus. At the end of the year, they will be a

valuable legacy from the Dome to the entertainment industry. The one hundred and sixty two strong company performs in rotation up to three times a day, seven days a week, every day in 2000.

1 Micha Bergese, left,
and Peter Gabriel,
centre, working in
the sound studio

2 Keith Khan, left,
works on the show's
specially created
props and costumes

3 Mark Fisher
watches rehearsals
in the Dome

4 The iron tower becomes an oppressive symbol of industrialisation

5 As part of their training programme, performers experiment with make-up

6 Performers suspend from mobiles

7 The Millennium Company was formed in 1998 following a UK-wide search for talented and committed young people

Body

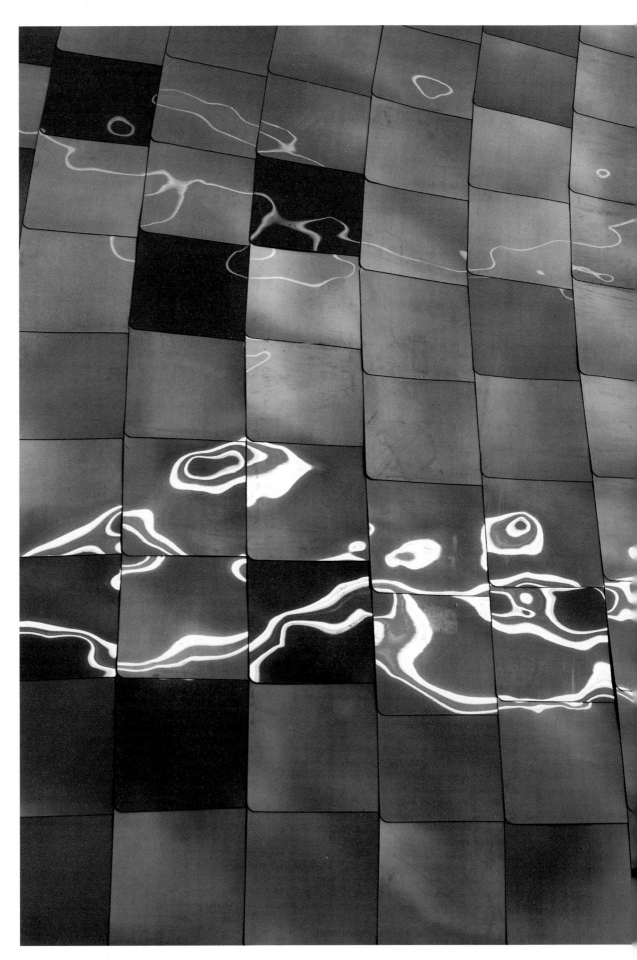

pp16-17 Shimmering lenticular tiles – over 88 000 are used to cover the bodies

1 The comedy-routine brain

2 The male and female figures in their gently reclining embrace

3 The massive pumping heart

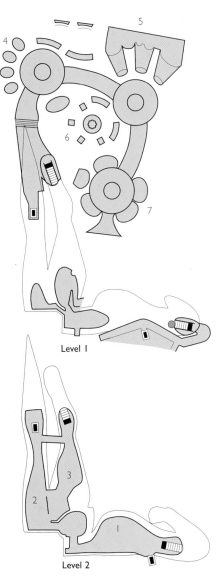

Level 1

Level 2

● Entrance
1 Heart
2 Eye
3 Brain
4 Perspectives on Beauty
5 Medicine and Health
6 Lifestyle and Well-being
7 Issues for the Future

Body is a spectacular, thought-provoking zone, instilling a sense of wonder at our bodies and at the prospects for health and well-being in the new millennium.

This zone is an imposing sight: part-building; part-sculpture. Two seven-storey high figures – one male, one female – lean towards us as they rest on one elbow. On our journey through the zone, we travel inside the embracing bodies and out to *Explore*, an interactive area at their feet.

As we enter the bodies, suddenly we are tiny, surrounded by pumping blood vessels just under the surface of the skin. This first part of the zone includes the chance to see our own skin close-up. It is just the beginning of an exciting and emotional experience.

We then move deep inside the male body through the right arm. Near the heart we realise – with shock – the power it needs to keep on pumping. Next there is a smaller, tranquil, womb-like space where shoals of sperm swim past as they race to fertilise an egg. Then a comedy-routine brain and a huge eye, staring reflectively at a wall of sad and heroic images, express the power of human emotion.

An escalator takes us through claustrophobic layers of bone, muscle, and epidermis, and we finally emerge through the foot of the female. Outside, *Explore* looks at three themes: how we fit into the world around us, how we feel about our own health, and what our hopes and fears for the future may be.

First, famously attractive people appear on screen to present different perspectives on beauty, and a range of people talk about the way they use their bodies to express themselves. A wall of telephone directories illustrates how much data is held in the human genome.

Next, in an area dealing with medicine and health, we see how medical care is changing, and what new drugs and techniques will mean to us, with the emergence of telemedicine and robosurgery. Exhibits include a mass-screening robot and the operating theatre of the future. Following this, an exploration of lifestyle and health looks at a *Keepwell* project for children and the concept of holistic well-being, dealing with issues including stress, diet and exercise.

Finally we discover issues that may affect the decisions we make about our bodies in the next fifty to a hundred years.

Body is sponsored by Boots, supported by L'Oréal and Roche

Mind

Level I

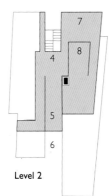

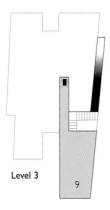

Level 2

Level 3

Mind explores the nature of our perceptions. The zone uses unusual combinations of art and technology to expand what we can normally see and hear. It makes us realise just how small is the spectrum of information which our senses deliver to us from the world in which we live.

This is one of the Dome's most architecturally daring zones. Made from huge bands which curve round on themselves and blur distinctions between floors, walls and ceilings, the structure appears to defy gravity. It appears to live and breathe with light 'nerve impulses' from optical fibres triggered by people walking on the upper level. This is an intriguing and maze-like building which confounds expectations as it takes us into

tunnels, corridors, chambers and wide-open decks.

As we travel through the zone we pass through four areas exploring different aspects of the mind. The first, in the entrance chamber, asks what a mind is and deals with issues of intelligence. Here we explore the complexity of a working brain using advanced scanning imagery. We also see a real-life colony of South American Leaf Cutter Ants.

The second area deals with perception and illusion, looking at how the mind plays tricks on us, as well as how technology allows us to see the world in new ways. There is an 'invisible' sculpture which can only be seen through infra-red cameras, an optical illusion, and a film called *Momentous Millennium* with sections moving at 10 000 frames a second.

The third area looks at language, how minds communicate with each other, and the power of collective thinking. It also looks at the role of communications technology in revolutionising the flow of information around the zone. Here we see a beautiful, responsive man-made life form called the *Neural Net Creature* and a 3D mapping of the internet.

The final part of the journey celebrates the potential of the mind. Here a film allows us to choose different futures and 'morphing' booths where we can change race, sex and age. They raise the questions about whether our sense of self is all in our mind.

Mind is sponsored by
BAE SYSTEMS and **Marconi**

2

pp20-21 The three metre high sculpture *Boy* reminds us that the human mind likes to ask 'Why?'

1 The 'morphing' booths challenge our sense of identity by transforming our image

2 The upper deck of Mind offers views across the Dome

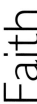

Baháʼí

Buddhist

Christian

Hindu

Muslim

Jain

Jewish

Sikh

Zoroastrian

Faith

Like a large tent where travellers meet, Faith is a stopping point on a journey through the faith landscape of the UK.

At the zone's entrance is a sculpture of a newborn child, with a short film in which children of different faiths share their thoughts about God. This reminds us that our spiritual journey begins in childhood. We pass by a graphic portrayal of nine major faiths practised in the UK which are participating in the zone.

Turning to the right, the impact on the UK of two thousand years of Christian history is explored. Practising Christians consider how today's ideas about justice, freedom, education and health care are still influenced by Christianity. They tell us who and what from history inspires them: an actress who strives to make accessible the story of Jesus selects *The Tyndale Bible*, the first to be printed in English; a human-rights worker identifies with the eighteenth-century black ex-slave Oluadah Equiano who campaigned in the UK for the abolition of slavery.

Straight ahead, we see how different faiths in this country mark key life experiences. Photographic stories on nine crystal pillars illustrate the distinctive perspective of each faith group. The creation of these photographs involved a major collaboration between faith communities which granted the photographers privileged access to their sacred ceremonies.

Following a display on religion's role in conflict and reconciliation, the first part of the journey ends as we hear reflections on death, belief and an onward journey from people of different faiths, as well as of no faith.

The next area asks 'How shall I live?' and gives some people's answers in a collage of images, illustrations and quotations. We are then invited to write a thought for the year 2000 and post it in a giant honeycomb wall. These messages will be sealed up for the next fifty years.

Night Rain inspires quiet contemplation and reflection as the colours slowly evolve

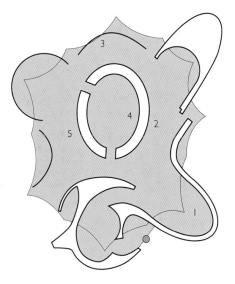

In the centre of the zone *Night Rain*, a light space, inspires contemplation.

Next, an evocation of the ways that faiths can act together is placed with a calendar of faith festivals in 2000. As we leave the zone we see ourselves reflected in the company of others whose faith experiences we have shared.

This zone has been developed with advice from the Lambeth Group (which has brought together the Christian Churches, members of other faith communities and the Inter-Faith Network) on the UK's millennium celebrations, and by individual members of the nine faiths represented in the zone.

Faith was made possible by generous donations from the **Laing Family Trusts**, the **Hinduja Foundation**, the **Jerusalem Trust**, the **Garfield Weston Foundation** and **three other trusts** and **organisations associated with the Christian faith**

A small section of
the *National Portrait*

1 The illuminated
collage of objects
selected by people
across the UK

2 *The Thug* caricatures
a less attractive side of
the national persona

Self Portrait celebrates British diversity at the beginning of the new millennium.

From the outside, the zone is a massive glowing circular drum. Revolving panels move across the structure's surface revealing images of hundreds of objects. These were selected in response to the question '*What one thing best represents Britain to you, something which you would like to take into the future?*' Thirteen thousand individuals and groups contributed and four hundred of their ideas are featured, ranging from fish and chips to the Queen Mother, from an Islamic Centre to Winnie-the-Pooh.

A rising walkway brings us into a huge space totally encircled by the *National Portrait*. This giant collage, three metres high and seventy eight metres round, has been created using over a quarter of a million photographs sent in from across the UK. It shows people set against recognisable but dreamlike landscapes of cities, mountains, forests and seashores.

Self Portrait is sponsored by **Marks & Spencer**

Next we encounter a display of what the UK people feel are their best assets – qualities including the 'British' sense of humour, creativity, inventiveness, culture and tradition. Within this a series of larger-than-life sculptures, both comical and satirical, offers a more critical view of the national persona and the weaknesses of society. The figures are in the tradition of British satire, from a comment about addiction to television, to an indictment of hidden racism.

At the centre of the zone a glowing, twelve metre high tube is encircled by steel reeds and we hear the voices of UK children expressing their hopes and wishes for the future.

Surrounding the zone we have the chance to learn from the contributors about why they selected particular objects. These people help us understand more about the challenging question of just what it means to be British in the year 2000.

Work

pp32-33 The monotony of regular commuting – as shown on the 'triptych' entrance boards

1 The clock ticks through the slow passage of 100 000 hours of an average working life

2 A huge table-football game promoting teamwork – one of the transferable skills required by employers today

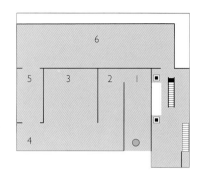

○ Entrance
1 The Old World of Work
2 All Change
3 Flexible Working
4 Laundrette
5 Dispatch Room
6 The Skills Workshop

We are living at a time of immense change. In the past decade there has been a spectacular growth in new, technology-based industries and many new kinds of jobs. An internet entrepreneur or a website designer had barely been heard of five years ago. At the same time, old certainties have disappeared. Working in a high street bank, once the safest job imaginable, is no longer so; technology has replaced bank tellers and branches have been shut. The zone explores this transition. It shows that work patterns have undergone a revolution. It challenges us to realise that, in the future, acquiring new skills and knowledge will play an increasingly important part in our working lives. This is why Work is connected to Learning, the zone above it.

Work begins by reminding us that the supposedly 'good old days' of a job for life often led to a lifetime of boredom. Inside a drab, grey factory are assembly lines and a clock slowly ticking through the 100 000 hours of the average working life.

Beyond this are sacks of shredded paper, the end product of the assembly lines which show the disappearance of the old world of work. Opposite, five thousand Post-It Notes – icons of the modern workplace – relay messages about new practices, like 'hot-desking'. They show how work is changing and becoming much less restrictive but also less dependable.

In the next space a display of fourteen outsize personal organisers reveals different scenarios from the new world of work when their screens are touched. Then in a laundrette there is a hanging rack of different uniforms. This represents the fact that far fewer people will have a single job for the length of their working life. Next, a dispatch room introduces the idea that we have 'core skills' as employers send requests for people equipped with necessary abilities and qualities.

In the final space, a range of different games test these skills – the ability to communicate, for example, or solve problems, or use new technology. There is the world's largest table-football game, a television quiz-style numeracy test, and a computer game where you have to pick up skills before the monster catches you.

An escalator leads to Learning on the upper storey.

THE AVERAGE PERSON WORKS 100,000 HOURS DURING THEIR LIFETIME

2

Work is sponsored by **Manpower**

Learning

pp36-37 Bookshelves with more than thirteen thousand familiar books entice us into the zone

1 *The Magic Seed* challenges our preconceptions about learning

2 The 'infinite orchard' shows us new ways of working

● Entrance
1 School Corridor
2 School Hall
3 Infinite Orchard

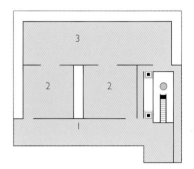

For the vast majority of people in the UK, education used to be something that stopped when they left school or college, but today this is no longer the case. Technological advancements and the changing face of work mean that employers need employees able and willing to acquire new skills. As the job for life has disappeared, so the idea of lifelong learning has taken hold. However, learning is about more than economic necessity. It is also an end in itself, giving enjoyment and fulfilment as well as opening up new opportunities and choices.

The escalator that takes us into Learning is surrounded by skills icons showing how acquiring new skills is an essential part of our working lives, and how the relationship between work and learning is constantly changing.

The zone is in three parts. The first is a re-creation of school life. A giant corridor, which may unsettle some adults, smells of boiled cabbage and disinfectant as lessons progress noisily behind closed doors.

When a bell goes, a door flies open and we are led into a school hall. Here a film called *The Magic Seed* shows how the life of a bored and disaffected eleven year old girl and her family is changed for the better by a wise old teacher. The film, which uses no spoken words, has a number of surprising and magical theatrical effects.

The third area of the zone is an 'infinite orchard'. Surrounded by trees and springy turf, fifty mirrored cubes equipped with computer screens take your image and make you centre-stage in one of a series of adventures. These all show new ways of learning. Above all, our experience shows that learning for life is key. As we leave the zone we see a real-life example of how technology is already helping children learn, share and communicate with each other using the internet (see *Tesco SchoolNet 2000* on page 83).

Learning is sponsored by **Tesco**

Rest

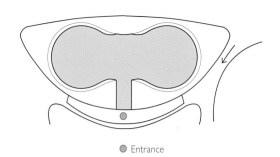

● Entrance

Rest's remarkable space offers us a moment of calm and tranquility

Keeping up with the pace of life today means we also need to be able to stop. Rest is a surprising and magical world: the Dome's relaxation chamber where we can go to escape and reflect.

The zone is a rainbow-coloured, smoothly curved shape set against a sea of black. Entering through a hidden, sound-absorbing approach, we step inside to experience deep calm.

We can stay as long as we choose, sitting or even lying down, in two sculpted spaces which are separate but connected by a single sky.

Rest creates a sense of peace by appealing to our senses. In this zone with no edges, no beginning and no end, beautiful layers of light and colour slowly wash across the sky. Gently evolving music loops through cadences at changing pitches and speeds. This original music, called *Longplayer*, was started on 31 December 1999 and is set to last through the next thousand years. No two moments will be the same in this strange artistic space filled with transient light and sound, where we also catch unusual refreshing scents as they waft round the space.

Play

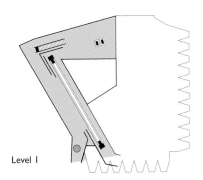

Level 1

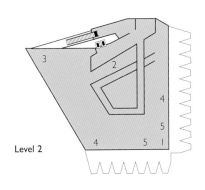

Level 2

● Entrance
1 Kids Room²
2 Armchair Goalie
3 Cats and Dogs
4 SofaVision
5 Kaleidoscope

Play is a fundamental part of life. It allows us to challenge ourselves, express our creativity and discover things we did not know we could do. With the advancement of technology, how we play is changing.

This zone has an unusual exterior. Above our heads protruding screens pulse with inner energy and life. As we enter, six sculptures make us think about the different kinds of play that are possible – from sport to leisure, music to the arts, hobbies to games.

Whether we play or watch the games in the zone, they are all designed to amaze and delight. As we move round the zone we encounter roving, technological *Play Guides* who capture our image and offer a quick visual sample of the seventeen games on a special screen.

Kids Room² allows children to express their creativity and discover new worlds as they take part in a storybook adventure, navigating down a virtual river to a forest where they dance with cheeky life-sized monkeys.

Armchair Goalie is a competitive game for two players. One kicks a penalty at a goal while the other tries to save it from the comfort of an armchair using a digitally animated goalkeeper controlled by a touch-sensitive console.

Cats and Dogs is a game for up to one hundred players. Two teams compete to protect the cats from a menacing dog called Mad Bob. Each player uses a 'magic wand' to move fences up and down and keep the rival animals separated.

With *Kaleidoscope* we make amazing shapes and music by moving our bodies.

SofaVision plays with our sense of reality; we seem to be sitting next to someone not physically there. We seem to touch them on screen, even scratch their ear, and yet we are never near.

On the way out of the zone we encounter again the six sculptures we saw on the way in. They have been transformed and are now animated with magical effects encouraging us to continue trying out new ways of playing in the future.

Talk

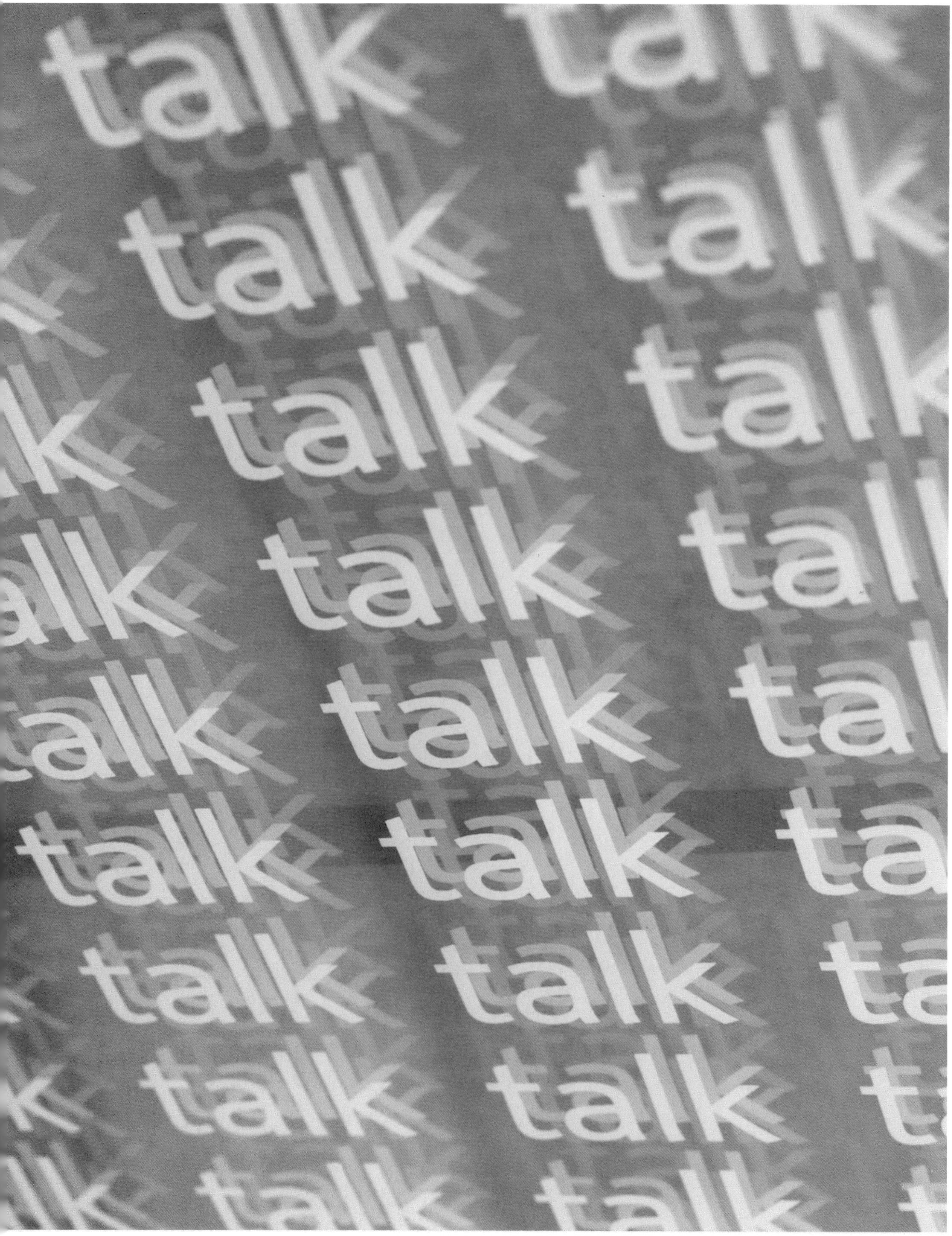
talk

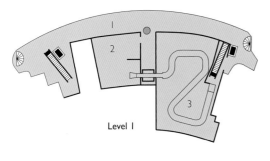

Level 1

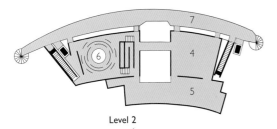

Level 2

- ● Entrance
- 1 Talktime
- 2 Talkworks
- 3 Talkwalk
- 4 Futuretalk
- 5 Talkscan
- 6 Talkshow
- 7 Talkdeck

This zone deals with communication; the most powerful and common of all human activities. Talk explores the human value of communication and the spectacular new technology promoting more and, hopefully, better communication. The structure of the zone expresses these messages: two sleek glass buildings lean into each other and, with pulsing light and sound, they talk.

Talk looks at the experience of communication and its place in our lives. As the ways in which we

have been able to communicate have become more sophisticated, we have needed to adapt to keep in touch. Recent technological developments mean that we are at the beginning of a new era dominated by information and knowledge.

By the zone entrance, a time-line shows the development of communication from 3500 BC to the present, from smoke signals to the internet. It makes clear just how much the speed of technological change is now increasing. The ground floor area explores how important talking

pp46-47 The sleek glass exterior

1 The dramatic entrance to Talkwalk, which reinforces the importance of communication in our lives

2 FutureTalk – a spectacular climax containing a tower of light, and where ET brings the experience to life

3 The TalkScan booths, where visitors can have their image scanned in 3D form, allowing them to download a personal 'avatar' from the web on their return home

is in our lives. Here we can listen in on private conversations, reminding us of the difference that talking makes.

After travelling up an escalator, we reach the kaleidoscopic FutureTalk area where we see examples of possible developments in communications technology- from a miniature videophone to an 'intelligent' pen that can download your handwritten notes into your computer at the touch of a button. We have our photo taken with ET and are given the chance to be scanned,

producing a 3D photo-realistic image which can be downloaded from the Internet later. We have the chance to send an email and surf the net using touch screen monitors that show how easy computer based talk is.

In a television studio style area, we see TalkShow, an interactive live show which invites the audience to give its views on a number of key communication issues and developments.

Talk is sponsored by **BT**

This zone deals with a universal fascination: money. It brings to life the link between our financial lives and the financial world around us. It shows that what we do with our money affects both the world and the value of money. A million people are employed by the financial services industry in the UK and yet most of us find it difficult to understand how money markets work. Generally, we see our daily dealings with money as isolated transactions, without realising that our bank accounts, mortgages and pensions link us invisibly to the global economy.

Money begins with a view of a million pounds; we enter a dramatic glass corridor lined with twenty thousand real £50 notes. As we move into the next area, we are invited to spend a million pounds. Using a gold 'spend' card, we must buy goods with our fortune in under a minute. Amazingly luxurious products are on offer: diamond-studded football boots, a set of solid gold spanners and crystal milk bottles. By asking us to choose what to spend a million pounds on, the game makes us think about what would happen if everyone spent their money in the same way.

The next area is the *Hothouse*, where the effects of this spending on the economy are shown. Until now, blue stripes and lines have marked the route through the zone, representing the flow of money through the world economy. After the intense

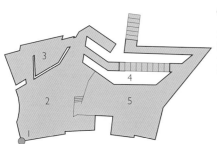

● Entrance
I See a Million Pounds
2 Spend a Million Pounds
3 Hothouse
4 Bridge
5 Invest

squandering, the flow speed increases until it becomes red and the pipes buckle and bend with the heat. The economy is now overheating.

A bridge takes us past an enormous montage of images showing world events such as earthquakes, multi-national company mergers and peace agreements. This is mixed with images of the financial markets which cope with this unpredictable world.

The next area is dominated by an image of the City of London; screens display live financial news and we can play an 'investing' game. As we start, our names appear on the wall as a sign that all the transactions we make interact directly with the City. On leaving, we are given the opportunity to find out more and feel we are in a better position to understand how money works.

pp50-51 Reflective bronzed tiles cover the thirteen metre high zone

I The *Hothouse* demonstrates the effects of our spending upon the economy

2 The zone lets us spend a million and try our hand at investing

3 The million-pound corridor

4 The exterior of the bridge

Money is sponsored by the **City of London**

3

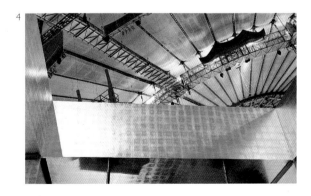

4

Journey

With its large fins and constantly flickering lights, the zone looks like a building in perpetual motion.

We pass through a *Motion Control Tower* – a communications hub with a number of exhibits, including periscopes through which we can see people around the world and in the Dome making journeys. Once inside the zone we are asked to give our views about transport on video screens and we see a film that reminds us of the strength of emotions that travelling evokes.

Next, as we move up a ramp, we travel through a history of people in motion. This multi-layered presentation includes artefacts, quotes and film footage, set against a graphic timeline. It bridges Iron Age canoe to supersonic Concorde.

As we reach the end of the ramp, the optimism of the past has been replaced with anxiousness and disorientation. This is today: the world is approaching gridlock. We move from this into a calm space encouraging us to pause for a moment and look forward to a future when travel is better organised.

We are given an introduction to the detailed possibilities of a positive transportation future. This area shows that successful solutions will require designers, governments and individuals to work together. It has three themes: *Land*, *Water* and *Air*.

Land looks at the future of a range of transport from feet to wheels to rail. Exhibits include

pp54-55 The exterior of the zone looks like a building in perpetual motion

1 Carbon-fibre yachts are built to be strong and incredibly light

2 Transport of the future – the sky car will fly on aerial highways

3 Planes to fly between city buildings may be common in future

4 Motorcycles in the future will be light, fuel-efficient and aerodynamically designed

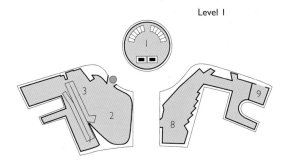

Level 1

● Entrance
1 Motion Control Tower
2 E Motions
3 Journey Through Time
4 Pause for Reflection
5 Journeys of Innovation
6 Four Futures
7 Tomorrow's Journeys
8 Time to Make a Difference
9 Virtual Journey

1

2

3

4

5

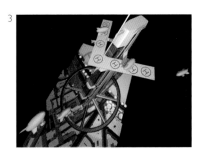

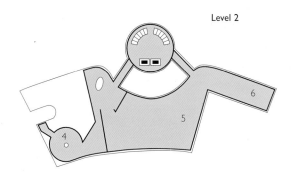
Level 2

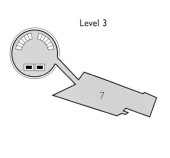
Level 3

5 Test your skills in the World Rally Championship car

future footwear, such as concept trainers and Kangaroo boots, as well as an ecologically designed and manufactured concept car.

Water shows new marine technology, giving glimpses of the future of travel over, on, and under, water. A full-scale submarine explorer forms a centrepiece.

Air looks at the development of air travel from Terminal 5 at Heathrow to futuristic aircraft design.

We can find out more about the future trends which are expected to affect transport planning in *Four Futures*. Then cross a bridge to a vision of a more mobile London, which challenges us to think about how the actions and technologies we have just seen could improve the future. We are invited to take part in interactive debate and to help solve a scenario of Edinburgh's impending traffic problems.

Shared Ground

This zone explores the importance of neighbourhood and community in our lives today. It is the Dome's giant time capsule, created using the voices of visitors during the year 2000 to provide an audio record for future generations.

Shared Ground is a twenty four metre high spiral building made from recycled card. It was constructed following a television appeal on *Blue Peter* in spring 1999. More than twenty three thousand children responded by sending in parcels of cardboard, and these were then recycled to make the hundred columns of the zone's twelve metre high structure.

The zone has three main areas: we travel up an escalator to the *Living Room* where oversize furniture senses when we are near and asks us questions. The sofa asks the question 'Who's the biggest couch potato in your house?' and, when a red light illuminates, we have the chance to record our response and contribute to the huge time capsule. This room makes us think about our shared experiences and how we live together.

In the next area we travel down a typical street. We walk past a lifesize theatrical set showing houses, a garage, a local pub and a park and we are asked to think about how we live as

pp58-59 The zone is made from cardboard sent in by children from across the UK

I Everyday objects ask questions about our daily lives

part of a community. Would you tell your neighbour if you wanted to paint the outside of your house a different colour?

Finally in the centre of the zone we find the *Time Capsule*. Here, amidst a maze of wires and connections, we hear recordings of people making their funny, intriguing and even eccentric responses to questions on their journey through the zone. We also see statistics analysing their reactions. We have the chance to listen and join in with people's discussions at different points around the zone using 'speaker tubes'.

As we leave, three terminals around the edge of the zone give us an insight into *Citizens Connection* – an on-line resource promoting and encouraging active citizenship (see page 83).

Level 1

Level 2

● Entrance
1 Living Room
2 The Street
3 Time Capsule

Shared Ground is sponsored by Camelot Group plc

Living Island

Most of us feel we have heard it all before: our behaviour is the cause of environmental problems and if we do not improve our ways, disaster will strike. We listen and feel bad. Some of us decide immediately that we will change, but in a little while, when the guilt has worn off, we forget. Mostly we do nothing because it is so difficult to see how our individual actions can have an impact, for good or bad, on the environment.

This is the difficult subject of Living Island, and yet it is a light-hearted and unusually involving experience. Based on a traditional seaside resort – sensitive to environmental damage but also loved by people in the UK – this zone has its own cliffs, lighthouse, beach, promenade and games arcade.

We enter Living Island through a sewage outlet pipe in a cliff face made of recycled cans, crushed and painted white. These cliffs are animated with flying seagulls and foghorns hooting at passers-by. To one side of the cliffs a machine manufactures pencils from crushed plastic cups, showing one unusual way in which waste can be recycled.

Inside the zone we walk along a promenade overlooking a picture-postcard seascape with a sand and pebble beach. This area highlights some of the environmental problems facing us today. Three palm trees show the effect of rising water levels caused by global warming: one tree has a rubber flotation ring

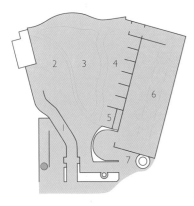

around its trunk; the next is shrivelled to show the effects of drought and the third bends over as though in a gale. In the *Jetsam Collection* there is a museum-style display of objects found on beaches around the UK.

The promenade then leads to the accumulator arcade, a large room of modified pier games. We can race against the clock to load a car full of passengers or fill a water-butt with a water pistol. Every game ends by telling us the effect of our game when combined with other visitors' actions. Here, against a backdrop of saucy seaside postcards on environmental themes, we see how each of our actions has a cumulative effect on the environment.

pp62-63 The Tunnel of Love, entrance to the zone

1 The promenade and life-guard tower

2 The environmentally themed carpet in the accumulator arcade calls us to action

3 Arcade games teach lessons about the environment

4 The peeled bark of the 'globally warmed' palm tree

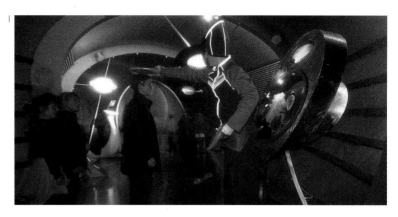

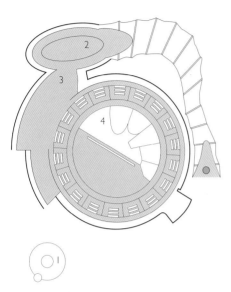

Home Planet invites us to travel to the most spectacular planet in the universe and sample its hidden delights. This zone has the Dome's only 'ride'; an imaginative, sensory experience of intergalactic travel in four dimensions.

Hovering outside the zone, alien craft circle the suspended globe and swoop down and look at us. Each of the four X-plorites embodies the spirit of exploration.

We enter the zone through a tunnel at the side of its curved, blue shape. Here, a spaceport called *InterGalatwick* allows us a glimpse of the future of travel. We take the *Hyperlink* to our departure spacegate.

Before we board our *British Spaceways Hypershuttle*, a short video programme welcomes us and explains the safety procedures. We then set off and data shields in our capsule display information about our journey. Gaia, our pilot, gives a commentary about what we see. She is accompanied by her son Max, who is full of questions and enthusiasm. When we reach our destination planet, earth, it is his wonder and excitement that helps us see our world through new eyes.

The front of the capsule opens up and we take a series of virtual visits to earth highlighting what is so special about the planet. There is some turbulence and temperature change as we move through air, water and fire to the earth's core.

Then as the capsule opens wider we come face to face with all life on earth, and finally we focus on humanity. On a huge screen we see a film, *Circle of Emotion*, showing people in different parts of the planet in moments of happiness, sadness, anger and love. We see these individuals and groups as part of the global community of humankind.

We arrive back at the huge, rotating globe. Here we are able to explore the planet further. We can discover the many ways in which the people of the world are connected, and, if we work together with other people, we see that we can even turn the world.

Home Planet is sponsored by **British Airways** and **BAA**

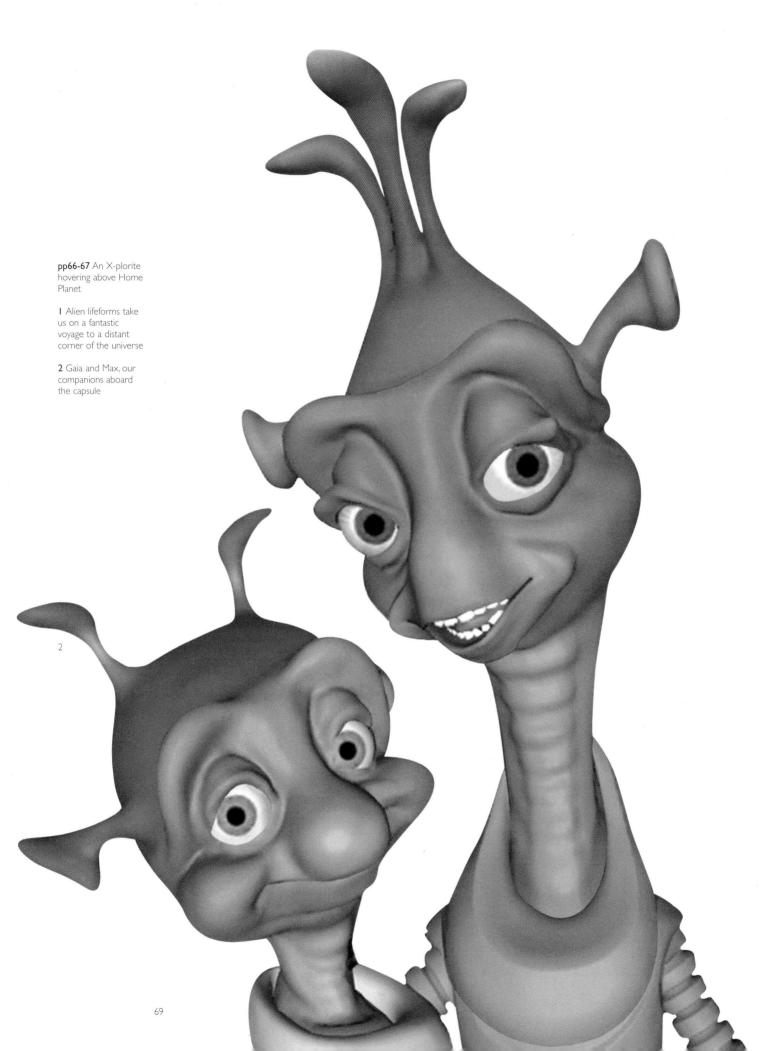

pp66-67 An X-plorite hovering above Home Planet

1 Alien lifeforms take us on a fantastic voyage to a distant corner of the universe

2 Gaia and Max, our companions aboard the capsule

2

Other attractions

Millennium Map

Located inside the Dome's main entrance, this thirteen metre high orange map shows the range and extent of Millennium Commission initiatives around the UK. Pressure-sensitive pads allow us to make the map light up in six different ways showing the new developments that have been funded, ranging from new construction and regeneration projects to activities uniting communities. **Millennium Map** is presented in association with the **Millennium Commission**

3 The Map shows projects 'Happening everywhere' around the UK

3

Timekeepers of the Millennium

As we step through the Stonehenge entrance we realise that this is the home of Coggs and Sprinx, the Dome's two timekeepers; young members of an alien race whose job it is to keep the wheel of time moving. These two characters have spent the last few months trying to put right the universe's time machine which they accidentally broke, as viewers of the television series will know. Luckily for us, they managed to collect the twelve crystals which power the machine and have returned to their home here at the Dome. The space is full of things collected on their travels, like the DaVinci flying bicycle with its special wings. A separate prehistoric area with a dinosaur, volcano and lava pads is just for toddlers.

Coggs and Sprinx appear on monitors to ask us to help them keep the time machine going by filling it with bits of time – in the shape of foam balls – and it is in doing this that we realise that the blasters and fountains have amazing secret effects.

This play area, which is located opposite the Play zone, is the first of its kind in the UK, and has been created with new technology from the US.

Festival of Britain Bus

Parked unexpectedly under a bridge opposite the Play zone is a red double-decker bus. The bus is a startling reminder of the scale of our surroundings: it would take eighteen thousand buses like this to fill the Dome.

A veteran of the 1951 Festival of Britain, this is an original *Ambassador Tour Bus* which travelled around Europe before the exhibition opened to encourage people to visit. The bus spent the five months of the Festival on display outside the exhibition on London's South Bank.

4

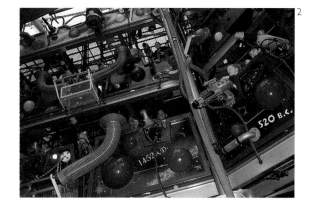

1 Coggs and Sprinx, the accident-prone Timekeepers of the Millennium

2 The fun-filled home of Coggs and Sprinx

2

Looking Around

From Beckton Ski Slope in the east to Battersea Power Station in the west; this hidden installation near Living Island is a spectacular three hundred and sixty degree view from the top of the Dome roof which shows its position in London.

5

Childhood Cube

Near the Blackwall Tunnel vent a two metre high cube offers glimpses of childhood imagination through a network of tiny, perspex rooms.

Over sixty children contributed ideas – the rooms could be made of anything, contain anything and be located anywhere in the universe. The magical miniature worlds which we see here were inspired by their drawings and hand-made with the assistance of the children.

Childhood Cube was created by Sarah Raphael

The Millennium Coin Minting Press

A fully working mint opposite Money produces *Millennium Coins* throughout the year 2000.

The glass walls around the press and cameras inserted next to the pressing dies give a close-up of the process of minting coins, from the insertion of blanks to the inspection of the coins by skilled operators.

Millennium Coins are legal tender – they have a face value of £5 – but they are likely to be kept rather than spent. Just as at the 1951 Festival of Britain, these coins are collectors' items. Their production and special Dome mint-mark makes them a limited edition available only at the Dome, which many people will want to keep as a memento.

The Millennium Coin Minting Press is presented in association with the **Royal Mint**

6

The Millennium Jewels

These twelve spectacularly beautiful diamonds are revealed during a light show using the latest laser technology.

The centrepiece of the exhibition is the two hundred and three carat *Millennium Star*, the largest top colour, internally and externally flawless, pear-shaped diamond in the world.

There are also eleven exceptionally rare blue diamonds weighing a total of one hundred and eighteen carats, ranging in size from five carats to the twenty seven carat *Heart of Eternity*, an amazingly vivid blue diamond.

The Millennium Jewels are presented by **De Beers**

4 The last touring bus from 1951

5 *Childhood Cube* shows the fantastic freedom of children's imagination

6 The *Millennium Coin*, specially minted at the Dome

7 The *Millennium Star*

1 Communities from across the UK will perform on the Our Town Stage during the year 2000

2 17th March: Kids from Northern Ireland tell their colourful and uplifting story

3 25th January: A piper and drummers visit the Dome for Edinburgh's Our Town Story

4 23rd March: Suffolk performers on the Our Town Stage

Our Town Stage

As part of the National Programme, *McDonald's Our Town Story* invites every community in the UK to create its own millennial celebration. This nationwide project, involving hundreds of thousands of local people, has been co-ordinated by education authorities and library boards.

Each participating community has its own day at the Dome. Local people will perform a twenty minute show three times a day on *McDonald's Our Town Stage*. The eye-catching outer structure is visible from across the Dome. Its seven, thirty metre tall, spectacular pink fabric spikes are suspended from the Dome's roof. They create a light-controlled space for performances on one of the UK's widest stages, equipped with video facilities to record all performances.

Merthyr Tydfil in Wales has been creating a pageant celebrating two thousand years of the town's history. School-children from Tyrone in Northern Ireland have been writing, illustrating and printing their own local dialect stories. Walsall has established a youth parliament, as well as creating an environment and heritage project, a CD-Rom, an exhibition and, of course, its performance for the Dome.

Stirling in Scotland was selected to be the first town to perform, on 5 January 2000. The town agreed to concentrate on its social history. They decided upon the ingenious idea of presenting their story with a cast of one hundred people as a dance attended by characters who step forward to tell stories from the town's past, present and future. The wide-ranging projects developed in addition to Stirling's performance have proved extremely popular. Music, art and dance workshops were set up, a CD-Rom created, and an anthology of writing by local children produced.

Different communities have approached the project in very different ways, but all the performances promise to be entertaining, original and fun.

Our Town Stage is sponsored by **McDonald's**

5 & 6 Some of the bizarre characters you might meet at the Dome

There are some strange and unexpected people at the Dome. These characters – like the friendly twelve metre high aliens who have recently arrived from a distant galaxy to celebrate the millennium with us, or the figure suspended under a giant, helium-filled balloon soaring to the innermost heights of the Dome – are not visitors; they are the Dome's live performers, resident throughout the year.

Performing around the Dome site are companies including professional jugglers, a collection of bizarre characters with clocks instead of heads,

re-enactments of the past and creations of life in the year 2020. On stage in *The Round* a band plays their own musical tribute to the British obsession with the weather, and in the summer a varied programme of performances will take place on the *Meridian Festival Stage*.

There is also an ongoing programme of world events, celebrating the diversity of world culture and tradition through music, dance and performance: from a Chinese kite-flying contest to a virtual-reality orchestra from Finland.

Street entertainment

5

6

In contrast to the smoothly curved Dome, Skyscape is a dramatic silver building with futuristic roof sails. This is the Dome's spectacular entertainment venue.

By day Skyscape is included within the entry ticket as a key part of the visitor's experience. From the moment of entering the foyer, innovative, multi-screen entertainment and live comedy provides laughter and sometimes unexpected reactions. The cinemas will show the specially written British comedy *Blackadder Back and Forth*.

By night Skyscape is London's newest entertainment venue. A huge stage will host separately ticketed performances throughout the year 2000. Skyscape will be a venue for established and emerging talent. It will host star-studded premieres and award ceremonies, live comedy, dance, cabaret, and opera, as well as gigs and concerts by new and world-famous artists. At these times, Skyscape's bar on the mezzanine level will be open with its stunning views of the Dome and the River Thames.

Following the huge success of the television series *Blackadder*, and after a ten-year break, the

1 Rowan Atkinson as Blackadder

2 Tony Robinson as Baldrick

3 Kate Moss as Maid Marion

4 Rik Mayall as Robin Hood

5 The futuristic roof sails of Skyscape

Skyscape is hosted by **Sky Television**

writers have been persuaded to create a wholly new story for Edmund Blackadder and his disgusting servant Baldrick. In *Blackadder Back and Forth*, Baldrick overcomes severe difficulties, including stupidity and personal hygiene problems, to create a home-made time machine. Their maiden voyage is, as we would expect, not the perfect 'cunning plan' they hope for.

As Baldrick and Blackadder try to operate the temperamental controls to get themselves home in time for the new millennium, they accidentally go on a tour of UK history and create chaos along the way.

Blackadder Back and Forth stars Rowan Atkinson and Tony Robinson, as well as Blackadder veterans such as Stephen Fry, Hugh Laurie, Tim McInnerny

and Miranda Richardson. In addition, a variety of guest stars appear, including Colin Firth as Shakespeare, Rik Mayall as Robin Hood and Kate Moss as Maid Marion.

Skyscape

1 The *Meridian Quarter* is crossed by the Prime Meridian

2 The new transport interchange is one of the biggest stations in Europe

3 Silver birch trees *(Betula utilis)* form part of the *Living Wall's* vertical garden

4 The *Hanging Gardens*, another vertical garden, is a natural meeting point at the entrance of the Dome

5 The reed beds in the two hectares of newly created wetlands hark back to the marsh-bound origins of the peninsula

6 The Royal Naval College housed the Dome's Greenwich Visitor Centre from 1997 to 1999

7 The *Cutty Sark*, part of Greenwich's maritime heritage

8 Water hoppers located around the edge of the Dome collect the rainwater which falls on the roof for recycling

9 The six hundred square metre *Ordnance Jetty* is a new haven for birds in the Thames

10 Kiwi flax *(Phormium tenax)*, on the north and west faces of the *Hanging Gardens*, makes dramatic sounds in the wind

11 *Blackwall Beach*, a new intertidal foreshore for the Dome

12 Scientists are monitoring the water use of the seven million visitors to help find better ways of conserving water in the future

Outside the Dome

Meridian Quarter

The large sweep of land to the north of the Dome is called the *Meridian Quarter*. This open riverside landscape offers impressive views up and down the River Thames. Canary Wharf tower is just a kilometre away across the river, and it is here that we can stand back and see the Dome structure.

As well as featuring diverse and sometimes unexpected installations, the *Meridian Quarter* demonstrates the main reasons that the Dome is in Greenwich. The area is crossed by the *Meridian Line* and the Dome sits in a newly created landscape – the product of the regeneration of the Greenwich peninsula.

Greenwich Pavilion

This curved steel and glass building, which sits between the hard and the soft landscape in the *Meridian Quarter*, houses both an exhibition putting the Dome in context and a café giving us a chance to sit and enjoy the Thames-side view.

The three-part exhibition uses models, illustrations, detailed visual panels, time-lapse footage and a specially created 3D film to complement the impressive setting.

The first section explains how Greenwich came to be the Home of Time, which is one of the main reasons that it was chosen to be the focus of the millennium celebrations. Here a world map is cut into time zones and the *Meridian Line*, cutting across the centre of these zones, continues along the floor like the Line itself, just a few metres outside the building to the west.

The second part of the exhibition shows the creation of the Dome. It explains how the shape of the Dome was a response to the curved shape of the peninsula, the climate, timescale and the need to create an economic yet festive and memorable structure. A short time-lapse film shows the Dome under construction. Linked with this, a dedicated area shows a 3D animation which moves from outer space down to the Dome.

The final element of the exhibition is an exploration of the likely impact on the local area around the Dome and the regeneration of the Greenwich peninsula. A large map shows the result of two thousand years of development in London and how recent changes are improving the eastern area following its decline. Panels explore the history of Greenwich and Woolwich and how new jobs and training are transforming the local area.

Greenwich Pavilion is sponsored by **The Woolwich** and **London Borough of Greenwich**

The new landscape

The *Meridian Quarter* is a newly created environment which will gradually develop over time. In the seventeenth century it was a tidal floodplain called *Bugsby's Marsh*. The land was drained for use and later contaminated by industrial processes such as gas refining. The clean-up which took place as part of the construction of the Dome made it possible to rethink what the landscape could be.

The approach aims to challenge traditional attitudes about public spaces. The area outside the Dome needs to accommodate large numbers of people and be used through two winter periods. The approach to planting is pragmatic, ranging from long-term projects to short-term installations. The *Meridian Quarter* has a hard surfaced area for large gatherings and summer shows. There is also a long-term, newly planted landscape of wetlands accessed by a series of boardwalks. The six acres work as a whole and are linked to landscaping further down the peninsula.

The wetlands recreate the landscape which originally existed on the peninsula. The area is planted with indigenous and naturalised species, hardy enough to survive the exposed local conditions and with the environmental benefit of attracting and supporting the widest range of wildlife. As the area develops it will become an interesting and living habitat.

watercycle

Watercycle

The wetlands area is an environment adapted to modern needs. The reedbeds act as a biological filter for rainwater collected from the Dome's roof. The complex root system of the reeds (*Phragmites australis*) filters and cleans the water before recycling.

The landscape is just one part of a larger *Watercycle* system to reclaim water on the Dome site. A transparent structure in the *Living Wall* allows us to walk under a waterfall and see into the treatment plant. Rotating panels explain why water supplies are under increasing pressure and illustrate *Watercycle* at the Dome. The water treatment plant cleans water collected from the roof, washhand basins and a borehole. It is then used to flush the nine hundred toilets on site, saving thirty million flushes through the year. Finally the Dome's toilet waste is converted into *ecotricity* (green electricity) as part of a model for sustainable water and energy use.

Watercycle is sponsored by Thames Water

Blackwall Beach

As part of the regeneration of the peninsula some sections of the Dome site's river wall needed to be replaced. Taking a challenging approach to the landscaping, space was given back to the Thames and an attractive view created over the river. Instead of simply replacing the steel sheet piling, the new defences gradually step down into the river. This creates a number of different habitats between tides and supports a large range of fish, birds and insects. The new foreshore is named *Blackwall Beach* after this part of the river which is called *Blackwall Reach*.

Ordnance Jetty

This disused industrial pier, formerly used to unload ammunition, has been turned into a safe haven for wildlife on the river. Using reclaimed timber and Thames driftwood to build a giant box on the jetty, and using plants from a site about to be developed downstream, this is the beginning of a long-term project which aims to encourage all of us to reuse derelict areas. Over time the planting will become much denser and new 'pioneer' species will establish themselves on the jetty. Water pools and stones have been added to attract ground-nesting birds which have very little natural habitat left on the Thames.

Living Wall

The boundary wall of the site has been turned into a vertical garden linking the Dome and the River Thames. The theme of the garden is water; a canal runs along its front and the garden's profile has been sculpted into a huge wave along its length. The coppiced willows and birch trees are more ornamental near the Dome, while near the river the garden becomes more naturalistic with mounds of turf planted with cowslips. This will evolve through the year as the logs from the winter of 1999 sprout in the spring of 2000.

Hanging Gardens at the front of the Dome

This huge garden is a green focal meeting point as we enter the Dome site at Main Square. It serves the practical purpose of screening the escape shafts from the tube station as well as reflecting and responding to the epic scale of the Dome's architecture. This graphic sculpture wraps plants around three sides of a structure, changing species on each face to reflect orientation and creating a dramatic planting installation.

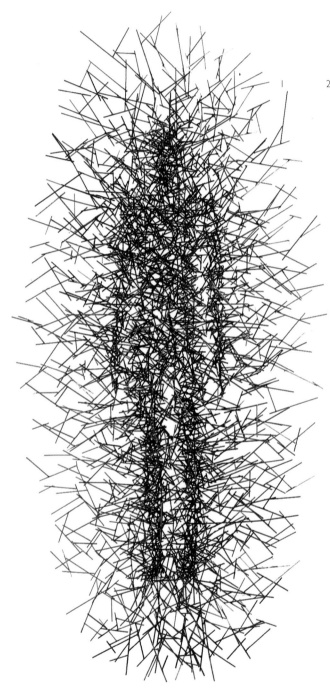

Sculpture

There are a number of arresting and unusual works of art on the Dome site. Created in response to the environment and located in the landscape by each artist, these are very individual and thought-provoking pieces. Seven of the pieces are by well-known international artists and one has been selected from the ranks of the young and unknown.

Life Time

Located on the *Meridian Quarter's* piazza, this three-part sculpture shows faces and profiles when looked at from certain angles. The centrepiece is over seven metres tall and the sculpture is constructed from carbon-kevlar, a new high performance material used in the manufacture of yachts.

Tony Cragg is one of Britain's best-known artists; he won the Turner Prize in 1988

Friday/Saturday

This sound sculpture reflects the seafaring history of the Thames and the importance of Greenwich to worldwide shipping. The sculpture uses each of the octagonal faces of the Blackwall Tunnel vent next to the *Meridian Line* to emit sounds from different ports around the world in their given time zone, twenty four hours a day.

Tacita Dean was nominated for the Turner Prize in 1998

Slice of Reality

An ingenious response to the Dome's riverside location and to the 'slicing' of the *Meridian Line* through the site; this sculpture sits in the Thames itself. This vertical cross-section of a ship from bridge to hull is a celebration of merchant shipping on the Thames.

Richard Wilson is well-known for cutting and slicing architectural forms; he was nominated for the Turner Prize in 1988

Parabolic Waters

This massive mirrored form reflects the sky and draws the viewer into its seemingly still reflection. Located near the *Greenwich Pavilion*, this feat of engineering and art extends the artist's exploration of mirrored objects.

Anish Kapoor won the Turner Prize in 1991

It Pays to Pray

Four adapted vending machines on the riverside walk each display LED 'prayers', inspired by the names of chocolate bars, for twenty pence (which is returned at the end).

Rose Finn-Kelcey's work was included in Kassel Dokumenta in 1992

Skyline

This giant lightline in space forms moving blue writing in the air over the wetlands.
Bill Culbert is well-known for his experiments with light, including Skyline 2 exhibited at the Serpentine Gallery in 1996

Quantum Cloud

Near Skyscape, on the river approach to the Dome, a towering figure is visible in a cloud of over three thousand five hundred square steel tubes. This vision of the human being as a zone of light and energy is a new departure for the artist. The sculpture is the product of complex engineering and computer modelling work; it stands on one of the two remaining posts of the previous jetty.
Antony Gormley is well-known for Angel of the North; he won the Turner Prize in 1994

Awayday

Fragments of rollercoaster track evoke the pleasure and excitement of theme parks and funfairs. Standing nine metres high, this description of movement in space frames the view to the river from *The Round*.
Steve Bunn is a recent graduate of the Royal College of Art

1 *Quantum Cloud*, standing twenty seven metres high, shows the human form as a zone of light and energy

2 *Slice of Reality* is a vertical cross-section of a ship standing in the Thames

3 *Skyline's* argon-filled tubes can be interpreted as writing, music or a response to the open river view

4 *Life Time* continues the artist's exploration of themes through the unlikely juxtaposition of materials

5 One of the granite discs engraved with poetry from countries on the *Meridian Line*

6 The *Spiral of Innovation* takes us on a journey through Britain's creativity

The Meridian Line

The Prime Meridian of the world, from which all longitude is measured, cuts the north-western edge of the Dome site. Marked with red light, it slips into the River Thames and emerges to cross the wildlife jetty.

The area around the Line is raised and separated by a strip of water from the rest of the *Meridian Quarter*. This is a space from which to look out beyond the Dome and Greenwich to other places touched by the Line and to the perspectives, experiences and cultures of the people of the world.

A large mirror on the *Living Wall* takes the *Meridian Line* southward into infinity. This is a photograph opportunity as we catch ourselves standing either side of the Line and across time zones.

On the mirror is a map showing the eight countries which the Line crosses: the UK, France, Spain, Algeria, Mali, Burkina Faso, Togo and Ghana. Large granite disks on the ground either side of the Line are engraved with poems from each of the countries. These are by well-known and lesser-known poets, mostly still living, though some is traditional folk poetry. The poems are varied and rich, they take the form of riddles, songs, landscape poetry, sharp social observation and love

poetry and they make up a diverse reflection on life along the *Meridian Line* at the beginning of the year 2000.

Spiral of Innovation

Further along the river edge is another installation which also looks out beyond the Dome site. As we walk up the curving gradient of this three metre high spiral we journey through the UK's inventiveness, seeing and hearing about amazing *Millennium Products*. A selection of these examples of creativity and innovation is embedded in the surface of the *Spiral of Innovation*. They all improve our lives at the beginning of the new millennium.
Spiral of Innovation is presented by the **Design Council**

The National Programme and the Millennium Festival

The National Programme is a UK-wide programme of events and activities. It has been created to reflect the themes explored in the Dome, such as realising our individual potential, strengthening our communities, celebrating our diversity and preparing for the future. Each activity is closely related to a zone in the Dome.

The National Programme is intended to appeal to a wide cross-section of society and to make a difference in local communities. It will continue after the year 2000, as a key part of the legacy of the Dome.

The National Programme has created a new range of partnerships between private, public and voluntary sectors. Companies have extended their activity beyond traditional forms of corporate support for social, educational and community projects, and charities have worked collectively, some for the first time.

Engineering our Future sponsored by **BAE SYSTEMS**, linked to **Mind**
Encouraging school pupils aged eight to eighteen years to take an active interest in science, technology and engineering. It also aims to inspire young people to become scientists and engineers themselves.

Future Talk sponsored by **BT**, linked to **Talk**
A programme of children's workshops for those aged five to sixteen years, exploring what makes communication effective and the problems that arise through misunderstanding. It also features consumer literature aimed at adults.

The Common Purpose Citizens Connection sponsored by **Camelot Group plc**, linked to **Shared Ground**
An on-line resource for everyone, giving people the inspiration, information and tools to make a difference in society.

We're in Business sponsored by the **City of London**, linked to **Money**
Promoting business and enterprise by establishing the UK's first business 'Oscars' with a local, regional and national competition to find the UK's favourite companies.

Manpower National Skills Festival 2000 linked to **Work**
This initiative, developed in partnership with UK SKILLS and The Prince's Trust, aims to help young people succeed by promoting excellence in practical skills, generating high-quality jobs for the future. A nationwide series of skills-related events will culminate in the biggest ever UK celebration of skills in July 2000.

Children's Promise sponsored by **Marks & Spencer**, linked to **Self Portrait**
The most ambitious charity fundraising initiative ever attempted in the UK, which asks people to give one hour's earnings to a consortium of seven children's charities to provide a better future for the children of the next millennium.

Voices of Promise sponsored by **Marks & Spencer**, linked to **Self Portrait**
A project which invited every school in the country to compose a Children's Promise Song for the Millennium. Schools registered in October 1998 and fifty thousand children aged seven to sixteen took part. Twenty two songs have been recorded on the *Voices of Promise* CD under the supervision of Sir George Martin – the man who arranged the Beatles' songs.

Reach for the Sky sponsored by **BSkyB**, linked to **Skyscape**
A programme encouraging teenagers to realise their potential by providing practical and stimulating resources to encourage them to see what they can be. One thousand two hundred young people will take part in career workshops across the UK.

Tesco SchoolNet 2000 linked to **Learning**
The world's biggest internet project that has involved over fifteen thousand UK schools. It includes a 'Domesday Book' website database of contemporary life as seen through pupils' eyes at the start of the year 2000.

McDonald's Our Town Story
(see page 72)

The Millennium Festival
A partnership between the eleven **National Lottery Distributors** and the **New Millennium Experience Company**
The Millennium Festival, supported by Coca-Cola, distributed £55 million to individuals and projects around the UK in February 1999. In autumn 1999 £45 million was distributed in the second round of grant-giving. In doing so it supported over twenty thousand groups.

BAA Millennium Youth Games linked to **Home Planet**
Part of the Millennium Festival, this is the world's largest sporting event for young people with a Grand Final taking place just before the 2000 Sydney Olympics.

To find out more and get involved, call the National Programme information line: **0870 241 1999**

Faith

Rest

Self Portrait

Millenniu

Mind

Our Town Stage

Money

Learning

Work

84

Home Planet

Living Island

Shared Ground

Talk

Journey

Body

Play

Timekeepers of the Millennium

Millennium Map

Visitors enjoying the Dome

Hosts

In their distinctive yellow and black outfits, our hosts are easily recognisable throughout the Dome. They are here to assist you with every aspect of your visit, from helping out at the zones to working at the admission gates, the shops, the attractions outside the Dome and the Millennium Show.

The Dome's one thousand hosts reflect the diversity of the UK population in age, physical ability and ethnic background. They were all recruited with the help of Manpower plc, one of the Dome's Official Sponsors, through its network of two hundred branches. Anyone who wanted to work at the Dome, no matter where they were based, could go through the first stage of selection without leaving their home area.

Hosts followed a training course tailored to the exacting requirements of the Dome, through which they developed skills in areas including communication, self motivation and teamwork. The training was based around 'seven service principles' developed by the Dome's visitor services team.

Hosts are continually developing their skills through the NMEC learning resource centre. They have regular on-the-job training and can take part in a range of more formal training courses in topics including sign language, foreign languages and information technology. In addition, all hosts have access to Manpower's Global Learning Centre, offering them the chance to develop IT and management skills via computer.

Manpower is the sponsor of Work, a zone exploring our skills and choices in the future world of work.

The Dome, the nation and you

Rt Hon Chris Smith MP Chairman of the Millennium Commission

The Dome is, we hope you will agree, a magnificent achievement. It fully deserves the recognition it is receiving around the world as an international landmark building for the third millennium. The extraordinary diversity of its contents pays eloquent testimony to our nation's creativity and highlights vital issues facing us all now. There is also plenty of entertainment to provide a good day out for young and old.

A Millennium Commission Lottery Project

The Dome was built without a penny of taxpayers' money but nonetheless you may have helped fund the project. Most people play the National Lottery at some time or another; that is where the bulk of the money has come from.

The Millennium Commission is one of the bodies which distributes money raised by the National Lottery. In all, £2 000 million has been made available and this sum has been matched by funds from a wide range of private and public sources. As a result the total investment in new projects is £4 000 million. Just under twenty per cent of this has been spent on the Dome with the balance well spread around the UK. This guide identifies the sponsors who have also provided funds for the Dome. Without their generous help, what you see around you could not have been built.

The Dome at Greenwich is the centrepiece of the millennium celebrations. But the celebrations range far wider across the UK. In addition to the Millennium Experience National Programme, the Millennium Commission — with the other Lottery Distributors and the New Millennium Experience Company — is also supporting over one thousand two hundred Millennium Festival events which started on New Year's Eve and will continue throughout the first year of the millennium. This includes major events in twenty two towns and cities starting on the first weekend of the year 2000. The peak of the Millennium Festival will be that summer.

Throughout the rest of the UK the Millennium Commission has supported a tremendous diversity of projects put forward by local communities. They range from major projects such as national stadia for Wales and Scotland, eight new bridges, to seven new science centres and a new university.

On a smaller, equally important scale, there are also locally based projects such as five hundred new or rebuilt village and community halls. All will leave a lasting legacy. You can see the location of your local project on the giant map at the entrance to the Dome. But the Millennium Commission does not just create buildings, it is helping thousands of people achieve their potential. The Millennium Awards scheme will provide grants to forty thousand hidden heroes across the country who want to develop their own skills and put something back into their local community.

All these diverse projects, from the Dome to the village hall, are linked by the vision of people who have seen the new millennium as a time to make a difference. They deserve our congratulations for the immense amount of effort involved. The Lottery-playing public also deserves all our thanks.

Millennium Commissioners
Rt Hon Chris Smith MP (Chairman)
Dr Heather Couper
The Earl of Dalkeith
The Lord Glentoran CBE
Sir John Hall
Rt Hon Michael Heseltine CH, MP
Simon Jenkins
Rt Hon Dr Mo Mowlam MP

Former Commissioners
Rt Hon Peter Brooke CH, MP
Rt Hon Stephen Dorrell MP
Rt Hon Virginia Bottomley MP
The late Lord Montague of Oxford CBE
Rt Hon David Clark MP
The Baroness Scotland of Asthal QC
Rt Hon Dr Jack Cunningham MP

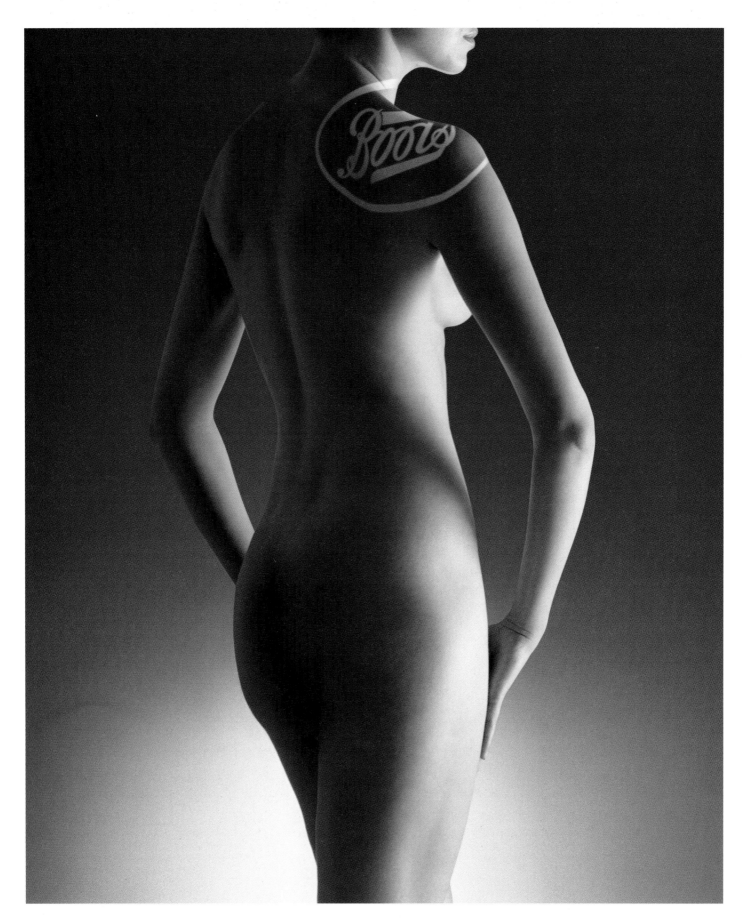

At Boots there's a health and beauty product for every inch of your body.

With BT FutureTalk the opportunity for better communication is out there.

Email, the internet, mobile phones, pagers, videophones, conference calling. The tools of communication change day-by-day, and it's important to know how to use them. Even more important though, is to learn how to make the most of the opportunities they offer - to communicate better with each other as human beings. FutureTalk, BT's Millennium programme, has been set up with exactly this in mind. The aim isn't to baffle you with science and technology but guide you through the various ways that you can enhance your own communication skills. There's our sponsorship of the Talk zone at the Dome, a travelling drama workshop helping over a million children become better communicators, our involvement with the FutureWorld regional exhibitions, and a wealth of literature that further illustrates new ways of staying in touch. So if you want to be a better communicator tomorrow, get out there. Today. Visit www.bt.com/futuretalk to find out more.

BT *Stay in touch*

The heart of world finance

Where money works

CITY OF LONDON

BARCLAYS   CGU
CORPORATION
OF LONDON
♻ NatWest Group   PRUDENTIAL   REUTERS   THE **WOOLWICH**

putt putt putt putt putt putt putt putt

1903

brmm brm brmmm brmmm

1950

varooooooooooooom

1990

vaaaaaaaaaaaa

2040

zeeeeeeb

2090

schnip

2150

 Journey

Official Sponsor

be the next billionaire.co.uk

I CAN

Don't miss the M&S Self Portrait Zone.

(After all, you helped to make it.)

Part of David Mach's National Portrait.

As Britain's largest high street retailer, M&S has played a leading part in the daily life of this country for over 100 years.

Who better to ask everyone in the country what they thought was special about Britain and why?

The result is a thought-provoking experience called the Self Portrait zone. There's a revolving wall with 400 photographs depicting those messages, and there are sculptures by Gerald Scarfe offering a more critical view of the national persona.

Encircling the inside of the zone, David Mach's National Portrait amalgamates over a quarter of a million photographs from people across the UK.

In the very centre of the zone, you'll be uplifted by children's voices describing their hopes for the future.

And at the end of your amazing day, the Self Portrait zone will have shown you a little more about your amazing country.

MILLENNIUM EXPERIENCE

Official Sponsor

MARKS & SPENCER

www.marks-and-spencer.co.uk

You could see them performing at the Dome.

As part of our commitment to local communities young people from all over the country will be given the opportunity to perform in the Dome. 'McDonald's Our Town Story' will encourage them to find out about their local community, then write and perform a story about its past, present and future. We believe that this investment in young people is also an investment in all our futures.

While we're on the subject of the future, take a moment to think about yours.

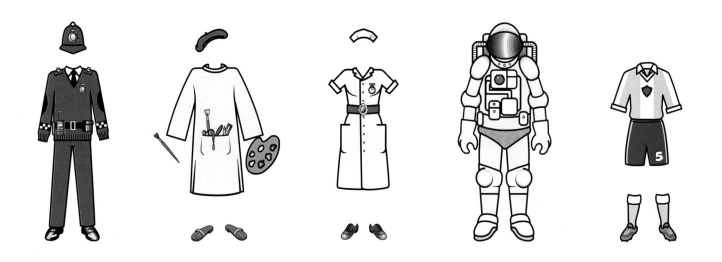

With an ever-increasing number of career opportunities available today, deciding where your future lies can be a difficult task.

As a young, innovative company, we at Sky hope to inspire you, Britain's teenagers, to see what you can be in the new Millennium.

That's why we've created Reach For The Sky. A nationwide initiative designed to help you discover and harness your talents and passions, to find a career that's right for you.

So take control of your future: log on to www.reachforthesky.co.uk.

Tesco is proud to sponsor British education.

We went on holiday from Stansted airport. There were lots of shops and cafes and nice people helping us all the way to the airplane.

Kieran Tickner, 6

BAA's Millennium Youth Games are really good. It's something for teenagers to get into. It gives kids an opportunity to be something and get rewarded for their achievements

Funmi Adenaike, 14

Mum and Dad are taking me and my brother to the Dome when it opens. I can't wait to meet the aliens Max and Gaia at the home Planet

Holly Jones, 7

BAA. The world's leading international airport company
Sponsors of the **BAA Millennium Youth Games**
Sponsors of **Home Planet** at the Dome

BAA Airports

Official Partner

GATEWAYS TO THE 21st CENTURY

HEATHROW • GATWICK • STANSTED • GLASGOW
EDINBURGH • ABERDEEN • SOUTHAMPTON

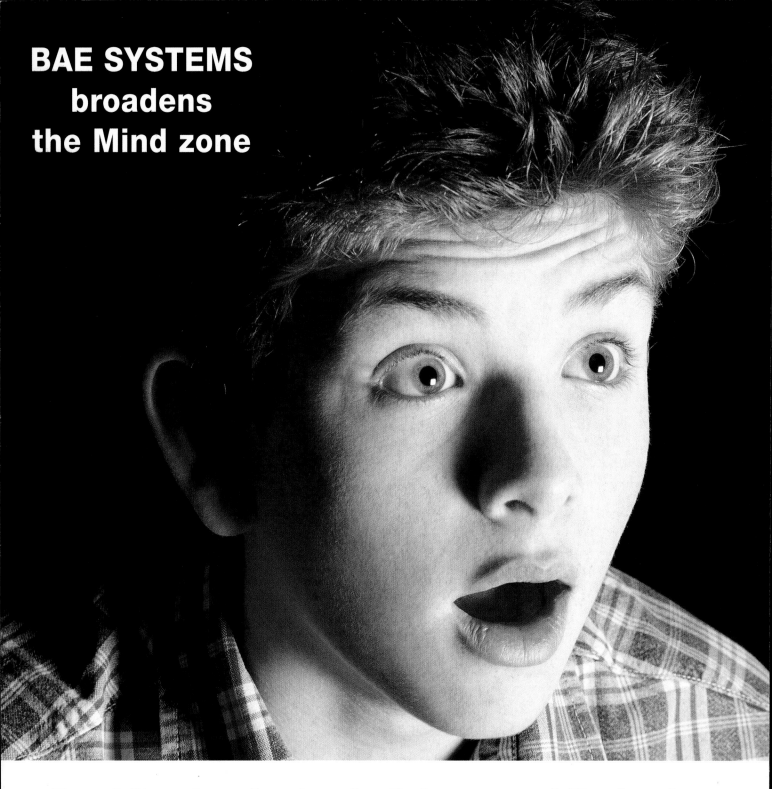

BAE SYSTEMS broadens the Mind zone

Providing Inspiration in Science and Technology

We want engineering to excite. We want it to stir the senses. To motivate. To challenge. To challenge convention. To confound the critics.

But most of all we want primary and secondary education to inspire a future generation of scientists, technologists and engineers.

To achieve this, Engineering our Future, a nationwide science and technology education programme has been developed as part of the Millennium Learning Experience. A highly innovative scheme that will not only transform perceptions of the subjects, but will highlight many exciting career opportunities.

We will also be celebrating the role of engineering in our lives through our involvement with the Mind zone in the Dome. Another engineering feat aimed at broadening the mind.

MILLENNIUM EXPERIENCE

Official Sponsor

BAE SYSTEMS

www.baesystems.com

Visit

all

See everything the world has to offer in the new millennium.

BRITISH AIRWAYS
The world's favourite airline

MILLENNIUM
EXPERIENCE

Official Partner

four

corners

Thanks a billion.

(Or, rather, ten.)

Many people owe you many thanks. Billions actually. That's because we aim to raise £10 billion for a range of Good Causes by September 2001, as a result of your participation in the National Lottery. (That's a billion pounds more than was originally hoped for.) So far, around forty thousand awards have been made to a wide range of causes through the National Lottery distributing bodies, so chances are, there's a project in your community that's benefited. To find out more visit www.national-lottery.co.uk

Camelot are official partners and ticket distributors to the Millennium Experience.

CAMELOT®
Operator of the National Lottery

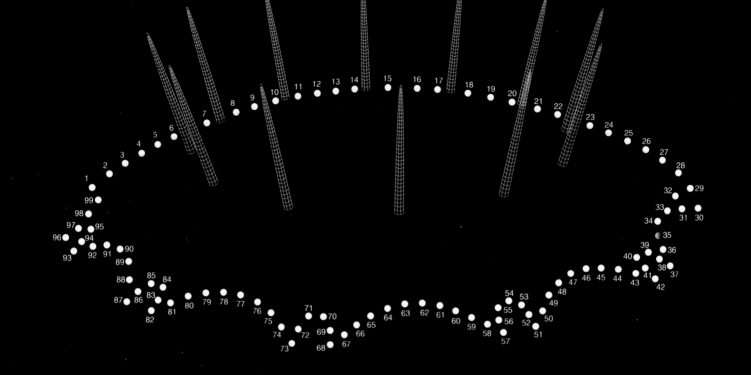

Unlike other showrooms, most of our wares won't be seen by a single visitor.

Yet the sharing of information is vital to almost every aspect of the Dome's operations.
From lighting the Millennium Show to catering, to event planning, scheduling, and admissions
for up to 35,000 visitors every day.

And making these systems work together to bring the Dome to life
is one of the biggest networks in Europe.

So although you'll see little of what we've done in the Dome, one thing's certain.
Without it, you'd see nothing at all.

More connected.™

3Com®
Official Supplier

MILLENNIUM
EXPERIENCE

It's so refreshing. Original and authentic. Makes my day. Everyday. Totally mouthwatering. The perfect drink. Thirst quenching. So uniquely invigorating. The unbeatable, ice-cold feeling. It hits the spot. 'The Real Thing'. There's no substitute. However you say it, nothing beats the unique, refreshing taste. Today, tomorrow and always.

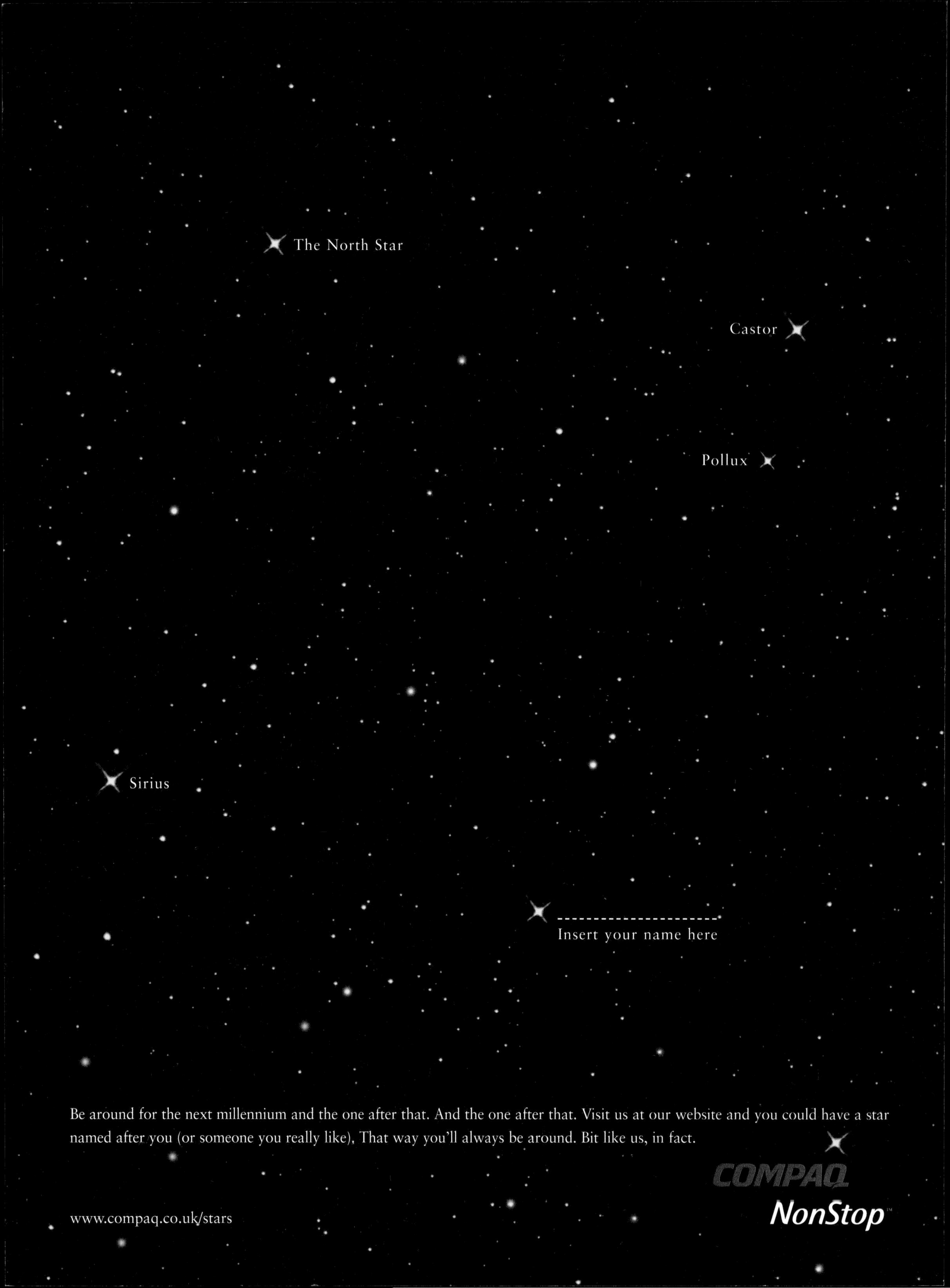
The North Star
Castor
Pollux
Sirius
Insert your name here
Be around for the next millennium and the one after that. And the one after that. Visit us at our website and you could have a star named after you (or someone you really like). That way you'll always be around. Bit like us, in fact.
COMPAQ
NonStop™
www.compaq.co.uk/stars

CONTENT FOR THE DIGITAL AGE

Daily Mail
NATIONAL NEWSPAPER OF THE YEAR

The Mail
ON SUNDAY

Evening Standard
Incorporating THE EVENING NEWS

FREE **METRO**

At last, England break losing streak

ASSOCIATED NEWSPAPERS LIMITED

W<small>HAT WILL YOUR FUTURE LOOK LIKE</small>?

(S<small>EE INSIDE FOR DETAILS</small>)

T<small>AKE</small> P<small>ICTURES</small>. F<small>URTHER</small>.™

Who knows, in years to come we could be on Mars eating Earth Bars.

Thames Water's idea for the turn of the millennium.

In the Dome, even the water will be 21st century. Instead of using traditional tap water Thames Water is recycling water specifically to flush the Dome's hundreds of toilets.

This is collected on-site from the rainwater falling on the Dome's roof, from groundwater rising from the Dome's own borehole, and from all the washbasins within. Recycled on-site, this reclaimed water is then used to flush the toilets without having to waste a drop of our high-quality drinking water.

Thames Water scientists are also studying new water-saving appliances such as dual-flush cisterns and infra-red taps in the Dome's toilets - all helping to find better ways of conserving water in the future.

We will even be producing the electricity to supply all the power needs of the Dome. This 'green' electricity is being generated as a by-product of our waste water process.

All in all, this will be Britain's largest ever water-efficiency project, providing us with a wealth of research information to help us to serve you, as well as the environment, better.

A flow of good ideas.

ONE DAY
I WILL BE ABLE
TO DRINK TEA
AS FRESH AS THE
DAY IT WAS PICKED

YOU CAN AT THE DOME

Official Supplier

At the heart of the celebrations.

DE BEERS

THE STONE
(actual size)

THE SETTING
(not actual size)

PICTURED ABOVE, THE WORLD'S MOST BEAUTIFUL DIAMOND. THE DE BEERS MILLENNIUM STAR.
ITS UNRIVALLED BRILLIANCE TO BE DISPLAYED - WHERE ELSE - AT THE DOME.

DE BEERS

A DIAMOND IS FOREVER

www.millenniumstar.co.uk

Building the Dome

1

2 3

1 Before the Dome, this peninsula was one of the largest 'brownfield' sites in Europe. It had been left contaminated and derelict by the closed gasworks and was in need of regeneration. Also cut by the Meridian Line, it was to be one of the first places to welcome the new millennium

2 Works began in June 1997. More than eight thousand piles were driven into the ground in twelve weeks to create the Dome's foundations

3 The steel masts were constructed in sections in the north of England, transported to site, then welded together

4 It took one of the largest cranes in Europe to lift the masts into position

4

5 The masts were placed onto four-legged bases which would eventually mark the main walkway inside the Dome. Each hundred metre high mast was held in position with steel cables acting like the guy ropes of the poles of a tent

6 Once all twelve masts were positioned, the individual steel cables which form the cable net were laid out ready to be lifted into position

7 The tension ring cables, which form the centre of the roof, were lifted in December 1997

5

6

7

10

8 The cable net was constructed in the air; outer rings with looped radial cables attached were connected together to form the roof structure

9 The edge of the Dome was built by stretching radial cables across the tops of perimeter posts, and attaching them to large cables connected to anchor blocks to hold the roof down

10 The world's tallest free-standing scaffolding tower was constructed to lift the central ventilation cap into place (also see page 108)

11 One hundred and twenty skilled abseilers worked in winds of up to twenty five mph, and at heights of fifty metres to attach the roof fabric to the cable net

8   11

9

12 Each mast contains a ventilation fan to refresh the air inside the Dome every two hours. The roof skin is made from two layers of teflon-coated, woven glass fabric, just one millimetre thick

13 Twelve cylinders round the Dome house the electrical power supply, back-up water tanks and pumps

14 Cables connected to the tops of the masts maintain the tension and shape of the roof

15 The roof structure of the Dome was completed in June 1998, having taken one year to build

Client New Millennium Experience Company (NMEC)
Architect Richard Rogers Partnership
Engineer Buro Happold
Construction McAlpine Laing Joint Venture

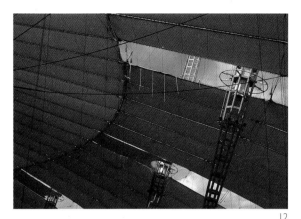

12

13   14

15

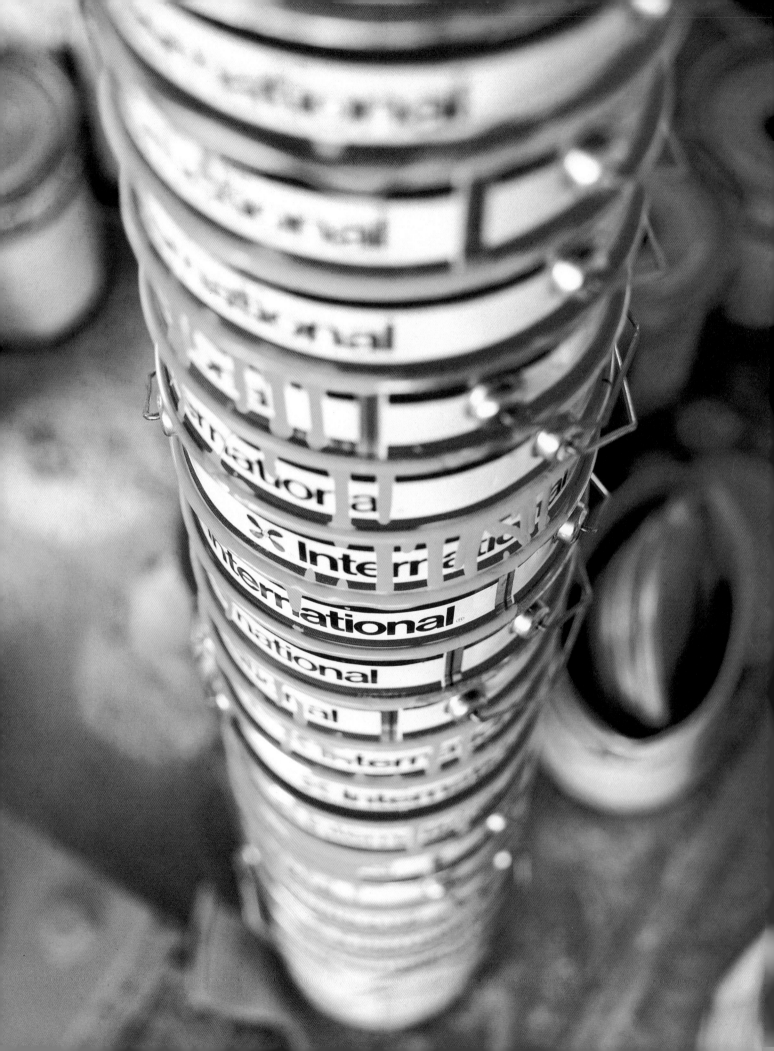

Creating the Millennium Experience

A vast number of organisations, companies and individuals have worked together as an extended team to build the Dome at Greenwich.

As we pass the vent for the Blackwall Tunnel we find a large installation listing the many contributors to the project. This series of six panels is a testament to the huge range of those involved: from the New Millennium Experience Company, the client body, to the contractors and the designers; from advisory groups to those supplying technical expertise and equipment and those operating the Dome during the year 2000.

Bright shades of red, yellow and orange give clarity and definition within the Dome

Behind the scenes

The installation shows the development of the New Millennium Experience Company over the course of the project and records the government and corporate support that has made the project achievable.

Starting as a small team, the New Millennium Experience Company became a client body for the construction of the Dome and the development and construction of exhibits. It then grew to a large company managing a National Programme across the UK and operating a visitor attraction at the Dome. All these changes took place rapidly, to an immovable deadline. The project has only been possible through the commitment of all the teams involved.

Building the Dome

A large number of the companies and organisations took part in the process of regenerating the peninsula, transforming it from a derelict site to the finished Dome we see today. Organisations range from those involved at the beginning of the Dome's history, like English Partnerships and WS Atkins which remediated much of the site, and created the infrastructure for the Millennium Experience, through to the companies that developed the concept for the Dome itself – Imagination, Richard Rogers Partnership and Buro Happold. The display lists the seventy two companies responsible for building the Dome on time and on budget, managed on behalf of the New Millennium Experience Company by the McAlpine Laing Joint Venture. It also give details of the companies which carried out internal and external construction and fit-out works.

Creating the content

A diverse range of companies was responsible for the design and development of the contents of the Dome. The list includes the Millennium Show team, the designers of the zones and other attractions round site as well as others who contributed to the process, including artists, sculptors, composers, writers, actors, model-makers, acrobats, street entertainers, film producers, and photographers.

The installation reflects the complexity of the creative processes, where there are designers of light shows, sound, graphics, software, costumes, props, special effects and multi-media working with companies responsible for the construction and installation of exhibits on site.

Lead designers of the zones

Branson Coates Architecture – **Body** structure
Caribiner – **Self Portrait** with Lorenzo Apicella at Pentagram, and **Money** with Bob Baxter at Amalgam
Eva Jiricna Architects with Jasper Jacobs Associates – **Faith**
HP:ICM – **Body** Explore
Imagination – **Journey** and **Talk**
John Hackney – **Body** content with Bertie Miller, Andrew McAlpine and Michael Cook
Land Design Studio – **Play**
Office of Zaha Hadid – **Mind**
Park Avenue Productions – **Home Planet**
Richard Rogers Partnership – **Rest**
Spence Associates with Shigeru Ban and Gumuchdjian & Spence – **Shared Ground**
WORK – **Work, Learning, Living Island** and **Shared Ground**

Dome facts

The footprint of the Dome is more than 10 times that of St Paul's Cathedral

It is wide enough to cover the Eiffel Tower laid on its side

The Dome is on the landing path of City Airport – a red aircraft warning light tops each of its 100 metre high masts

The air contained inside the Dome is heavier than the weight of the structure itself

The Dome is big enough to hold the water contained in 1100 Olympic-sized swimming pools

94 African elephants could stand in a straight line across the Dome

Advice

The Millennium Experience was supported by individuals and groups offering support, consultation and expert advice. This guidance was invaluable on such a massive, complex project.

The *Litmus Group* consisted of a selection of the UK's leading creative people. Regular meetings with the design teams helped shape the content of the zones. 'Godparents', both Litmus Group members and other noted individuals, acted as mentors to individual zones.

The *Accessibility Advisory Group* met regularly to offer support in the Dome's aim to become an exemplarily accessible, visitor-friendly attraction.

The *Sustainability Panel* met to advise on the environmental narrative content of the zones as well as review the site's practices and advise on activities as part of the National Programme.

The *Lambeth Group* brought together the Christian Churches, members of other faith communities and the Inter-Faith Network to advise on the UK's millennium celebrations.

Making it work

The Dome has had expert technical advice in all aspects of its development. An impressive list of companies supplied leading-edge equipment, systems and services making the Millennium Experience a world first in its scale and capability.

From reclaiming enough rainwater for thirty million toilet flushes a year, to designing extract fans in the roof capable of removing more than half a million litres of air a second, the Dome deals in big figures.

There are over one hundred square metres of light emitting screens as well as three hundred plasma display screens. Over fifty separate sound systems make the Dome the largest single sound installation of its kind ever created. The Dome's on-line ticketing system is the biggest ever created for a UK event.

'Smart' technology crosses many sectors, from intelligent vents at the top of the roof which close automatically when they detect rain to a system to collect our opinions as we move around the Dome. This system, called *Vote!* uses next generation 'barcode' technology for the first time at a visitor attraction.

In addition the communications to and from the Dome site use fibre-optic technology, carrying phone calls, computer signals and media broadcasts. The IT network is one of the largest installations in Europe, using twenty five kilometres of fibre-optic cable. Each cable is capable of carrying voice, video and computer signals. The Dome site's networked systems are all managed by a single solution provider.

Running the Dome

The Operations team had an early input into the design process, ensuring that the designers' initial concepts were developed into practical and workable solutions for such a large visitor attraction.

Following the construction of the Dome, many more companies and organisations joined with a wide responsibility from ticketing to looking after visitors including the two thousand hosts we meet as the Dome's public face. In addition to this, the team manages the operation of equipment and the maintenance of security, as well as the management of retail outlets, the cleaning of the site and dealing with waste.

To find out more visit **www.dome2000.co.uk**

Dome facts

The Dome could hold 1495 blue whales

The Dome could contain 175 billion sherbert lemons – if you ate one every 15 minutes it would take 5 000 000 years to finish them

The Dome covers an area more than three times that of the Coliseum in Rome

The Dome fabric is made of teflon-coated glass fibre and is just one millimetre thick

The Dome could contain more than 18 000 double-decker buses

Inverted under Niagara Falls, the Dome would take more than 10 minutes to fill

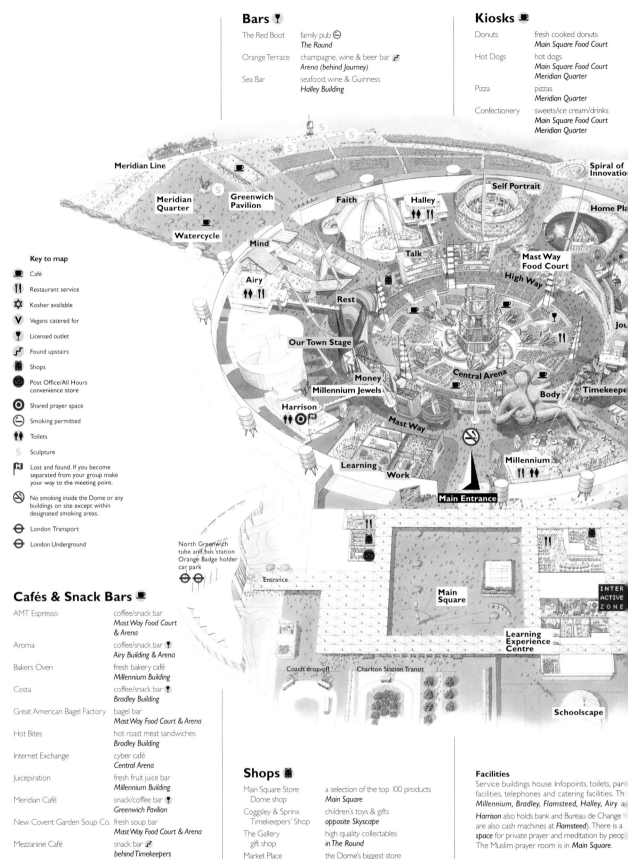

Bars 🍷

The Red Boot	family pub ⊖ *The Round*
Orange Terrace	champagne, wine & beer bar ♫ *Arena (behind Journey)*
Sea Bar	seafood, wine & Guinness *Halley Building*

Kiosks ☕

Donuts	fresh cooked donuts *Main Square Food Court*
Hot Dogs	hot dogs *Main Square Food Court* *Meridian Quarter*
Pizza	pizzas *Meridian Quarter*
Confectionery	sweets/ice cream/drinks *Main Square Food Court* *Meridian Quarter*

Key to map

- ☕ Café
- 🍴 Restaurant service
- ✡ Kosher available
- V Vegans catered for
- 🍸 Licensed outlet
- ♫ Found upstairs
- 🎁 Shops
- ✉ Post Office/All Hours convenience store
- ◎ Shared prayer space
- ⊖ Smoking permitted
- 🚻 Toilets
- S Sculpture
- ⚑ Lost and found. If you become separated from your group make your way to the meeting point.
- 🚭 No smoking inside the Dome or any buildings on site except within designated smoking areas.
- ⊖ London Transport
- ⊖ London Underground

Cafés & Snack Bars ☕

AMT Espresso	coffee/snack bar *Mast Way Food Court & Arena*
Aroma	coffee/snack bar 🍸 *Airy Building & Arena*
Bakers Oven	fresh bakery café *Millennium Building*
Costa	coffee/snack bar 🍸 *Bradley Building*
Great American Bagel Factory	bagel bar *Mast Way Food Court & Arena*
Hot Bites	hot roast meat sandwiches *Bradley Building*
Internet Exchange	cyber café *Central Arena*
Juicepiration	fresh fruit juice bar *Millennium Building*
Meridian Café	snack/coffee bar 🍸 *Greenwich Pavilion*
New Covent Garden Soup Co.	fresh soup bar *Mast Way Food Court & Arena*
Mezzanine Café	snack bar ♫ *behind Timekeepers*
Opa John's Famous Wrolls	Dutch/Oriental spring rolls *Mast Way Food Court & Arena*
Street Bites	snack/coffee bar *Central Arena (behind Body)*
t.fresh	tea bar ♫ *Mast Way Food Court*
World Bites	hot potatoes & fillings *Flamsteed Building*

Shops 🎁

Main Square Store Dome shop	a selection of the top 100 products *Main Square*
Coggsley & Sprinx Timekeepers' Shop	children's toys & gifts *opposite Skyscape*
The Gallery gift shop	high quality collectables *in The Round*
Market Place	the Dome's biggest store *next to Body*
Millennium Show Shop	Millennium Show CD & souvenirs *in the Central Arena*
Central Arena Shop	a selection of Dome gifts & souvenirs *in the Central Arena*
Post Office/All Hours convenience store	the Dome's own post office & general store *Main Square*

Facilities

Service buildings house Infopoints, toilets, par... facilities, telephones and catering facilities. Th... *Millennium, Bradley, Flamsteed, Halley, Airy* ... *Harrison* also holds bank and Bureau de Change ... are also cash machines at *Flamsteed*). There is a ... *space* for private prayer and meditation by peop... The Muslim prayer room is in *Main Square*.

Hospitality

All visitor service buildings offer hospitality an... suites serving 50 to 600 guests, with the exceptio... which can serve between 300 to 1000 guest... Club is located within *Acclaim!*

Opening Times

The Dome is open from 9am – 8pm. Please che... you book.

Restaurants

Acclaim!	à la carte restaurant	*Halley Building*
Fruits of the Earth foodcourt	healthy foods	*Millennium Building*
Harry Ramsden's	fish and chip restaurant	*Flamsteed Building*
Main Square Café	family restaurant	*Main Square*
Pizza Pasta	family restaurant	*Bradley Building*
Trade Winds foodcourt	world foods	*Flamsteed Building*
YO! Sushi	Japanese sushi bar	*Central Arena (by Journey)*
McDonald's	family restaurant	*Airy Building & Main Square*

Living Island

Shared Ground

Bradley

Play

Main Square Food Court

The Round

The Red Boot Pub

Skyscape

Millennium Pier

Map